The Twelve Houses of Astrology

The Ultimate Guide to Themes, Lessons, Birth Chart Interpretation, and the 12 Zodiac Signs

© Copyright 2023 - All rights reserved.

The content contained within this book may not be reproduced, duplicated, or transmitted without direct written permission from the author or the publisher.

Under no circumstances will any blame or legal responsibility be held against the publisher, or author, for any damages, reparation, or monetary loss due to the information contained within this book, either directly or indirectly.

Legal Notice:

This book is copyright protected. It is only for personal use. You cannot amend, distribute, sell, use, quote or paraphrase any part, or the content within this book, without the consent of the author or publisher.

Disclaimer Notice:

Please note the information contained within this document is for educational and entertainment purposes only. All effort has been executed to present accurate, up-to-date, reliable, and complete information. No warranties of any kind are declared or implied. Readers acknowledge that the author is not engaging in the rendering of legal, financial, medical, or professional advice. The content within this book has been derived from various sources. Please consult a licensed professional before attempting any techniques outlined in this book.

By reading this document, the reader agrees that under no circumstances is the author responsible for any losses, direct or indirect, that are incurred as a result of the use of the information contained within this document, including, but not limited to, errors, omissions, or inaccuracies.

Your Free Gift
(only available for a limited time)

Thanks for getting this book! If you want to learn more about various spirituality topics, then join Mari Silva's community and get a free guided meditation MP3 for awakening your third eye. This guided meditation mp3 is designed to open and strengthen ones third eye so you can experience a higher state of consciousness. Simply visit the link below the image to get started.

https://spiritualityspot.com/meditation

Table of Contents

INTRODUCTION 1
CHAPTER 1: ASTROLOGY BASICS...3
CHAPTER 2: MEET THE ASTROLOGICAL PLANETS 12
CHAPTER 3: NODES AND ASTEROIDS MATTER, TOO 29
CHAPTER 4: THE 12 ZODIAC SIGNS...41
CHAPTER 5: SUN, MOON, AND RISING SIGNS 57
CHAPTER 6: THE HOUSES I. EGO, RESOURCES, AND THE MIND 70
CHAPTER 7: THE HOUSES II. HOME, CREATIVITY, AND HEALTH........78
CHAPTER 8: THE HOUSES III. RELATIONSHIPS, GROWTH, AND TRAVEL..85
CHAPTER 9: THE HOUSES IV. CAREER, FRIENDSHIP, AND SPIRITUALITY..93
CHAPTER 10: PUTTING IT ALL TOGETHER: YOUR BIRTH CHART...101
EXTRA: ASTROLOGICAL SYMBOLS AND GLYPHS.....................107
CONCLUSION..110
HERE'S ANOTHER BOOK BY MARI SILVA THAT YOU MIGHT LIKE....112
YOUR FREE GIFT (ONLY AVAILABLE FOR A LIMITED TIME) 113
REFERENCES...114

Introduction

Have you ever wondered what makes you uniquely "you"? Astrology can provide some of the answers to that. It's an ancient science-based system that uses the individual positions of the planets, stars, and other celestial bodies to interpret the personality and potential of people.

Astrology is an ancient practice used to predict the future and gain insight into your life and personality. Many don't realize that by looking at the position of planets, stars, and other objects in space, astrology can help us better understand astronomical concepts. It forces you to engage with your world and its patterns in a whole new way, immersing you in the mysteries of the universe.

While you may not always like what this ancient art reveals about your innermost self, learning it can give you access to unique knowledge about where each planet lies as well as how all celestial bodies interact. If you're looking for a way to dive deep and get to know yourself better, astrology may be just the tool for you. It offers an array of fascinating and helpful insights into your life and even your relationships. With astrology, you can explore the positions of stars, planets, and zodiac signs at the time of your birth, or any other person's, and what that could mean. It can help you understand who you are and the possibilities inherent within.

Astrology can give insight into topics like understanding your relationships with others, discovering how energy works in the universe or comprehending the power of the seasons. Not only that, but it can be used as a tool to gain greater self-knowledge and explore life's deeper meanings. Astrology provides many opportunities to find knowledge, rediscover yourself, open your eyes to philosophies beyond the physical world, and see life from new perspectives. Who knows? You may even find astrology enlightening and eye-opening as you search for answers about yourself on this journey.

This detailed guide will explore astrology's foundations, from the planets and signs to the interpretation of your birth chart. It will go over the basics of astrology, such as understanding the meaning behind each planet and sign, finding out what it all means about your birth chart, and more. With each step, you'll better understand this ancient art and how it applies to your life.

Regardless of your knowledge level, this guide will provide the essential understanding and tools to interpret and navigate zodiac signs and everything that relates to it. Come on this journey to explore the skies and unlock the mysteries of astrology!

Chapter 1: Astrology Basics

In the modern era, astrology may be considered an outdated science. However, throughout human history, it has been used to explain everything from seasonal changes and celestial alignments to life paths and personality traits. Historically, astrological practices originated in India at least four thousand years ago and have since been used by numerous cultures for their own spiritual, religious, and medicinal purposes. The cycles gave them insight into their lives and held important spiritual connotations. Astrological calendars were even used to shape events such as agricultural harvests, military campaigns, and religious ceremonies.

The practice of astrology began in India thousands of years ago.
Wellcome Library, London, CC BY 4.0 <https://creativecommons.org/licenses/by/4.0>, via Wikimedia Commons
https://commons.wikimedia.org/wiki/File:Astrologer_of_the_Brahmin_caste,_India,_c_1825_Wellcome_L0035997.jpg

The shared human love of astrology links people all together, and it's been around since humans developed an understanding of the night sky. Dazzled by the mysteries out there, people tried to make sense of them in ways that still thrill people today. Many ancient civilizations sought answers from the stars and their arrangement in the night sky, from predicting events based on celestial movements to using constellations to create stories. You don't need to believe in astrology to admire its impact on human history.

This chapter will examine how astrology works, the basics of an astrological chart, and the debate of predestination vs. free will. It will then discuss the benefits of astrology, such as understanding personality, unlocking life lessons, gaining insight into life situations, and much more. Finally, it will look at how to interpret an astrological chart and how the interactions between the elements can provide us with life lessons and personality insight.

Introduction to Astrology

Astrology is an ancient practice that originates in the study of stars and planets and their influence on our lives. By understanding the relationships between various heavenly bodies, astrologers can provide insights into a person's life purpose, issues, successes, and challenges. The consultation process involves understanding the unique situation in a person's life as indicated by planetary motion. Astrology explains different areas of people's lives, from family issues, career paths, and health concerns to everyday attitudes and behaviors. All of this is essentially an attempt to make sense of inexplicable experiences to gain clarity and feel supported in moments of transition or uncertainty. Many people find comfort and guidance in exploring this ancient science. Astrological consults are becoming increasingly popular for people who want insight into life decisions.

The Basics of an Astrological Chart

An astrological chart is an incredibly powerful tool for looking into the future! It's like a crystal ball made up of mathematical and celestial symbols that can tell you what's ahead in your life. Understanding the basics of an astrological chart will provide insight into areas such as current influences, potential opportunities, and even things that may need extra attention. An astrological chart isn't something to be afraid of;

instead, it can be a unique and interesting way to explore life! With a look into your future, who knows what magical surprises await?

A. Planets

Learning how to read an astrological chart can be a fun way to gain insight into yourself and the world around you. Planets play an essential role in understanding birth charts and predicting the future. Each of the planets has its characteristics, with traditional astrology dividing them into masculine and feminine categories that express respective qualities like reactivity, transformation, and interconnectivity.

Sun signs are a significant factor in determining the traits of a person, while moon signs describe personality on emotional levels. The position of planets regarding each other reveals and activates the energies of that particular birth chart. Using this information, many believe it is possible to get insight into events from daily life to significant milestones. There is still much left to learn about astrology, but exploring the basics of reading a planetary chart provides a great starting point for enlightenment.

B. Signs

Signs are an essential component of reading an astrological chart. Astrology is a complicated language, with symbols and images representing our universe's different planets and signs. Each sign has its way of expressing itself, which is why understanding the signs can help you gain insight into yourself or others around you. At its core, a chart consists of pictures of circles or squares with labels that determine the sign in question. A chart also highlights aspects such as the expression of energies between each sign and will identify when there will be challenges or benefits during different times. With a deeper understanding of the signs, one can read their birth chart and gain insight into areas such as career, relationships, health, and more.

C. Houses

Houses in an astrological chart, otherwise known as beams or places, are an integral part of the chart-reading process. They act as lenses, allowing you to focus on specific areas of your life and providing insight into how they correlate to your overall well-being. Each house is associated with particular features such as planets, asteroids, signs, and elements. Studying these powerful indicators allows you to better understand your needs and desires and develop a deeper understanding of yourself and what you need to do to keep yourself healthy and content. If you're curious about the basics of this concept, it's never too late to start exploring. Learning the basics will give you a great foundation for furthering your knowledge from there.

D. Natal Chart

A natal chart is an astrological representation of a person's date, place, and time of birth. This moment defines and shapes who you are, how you think, and how you will interact with others. It reveals your strengths, weaknesses, gifts, talents, inclinations, and aptitudes. A natal chart can tell you how to approach love and relationships and your career path and even offer insight into life lessons you may learn throughout your lifetime. Although complex, understanding the basics of a natal chart can be empowering and transformational when used as a tool to navigate through life.

Predestination vs. Free Will

The age-old debate of "predestination versus free will" continues to be explored by theologians and philosophers – even today. On one side, those who believe in predestination argue that man is predetermined to a fate beyond his control. While those with the opposite view believe that our destinies are determined by ourselves and our choices. Both sides of this debate have their merit. While no definite answer has been reached yet, it cannot be denied that exploring this concept can further lead to exciting insights into your purpose in life and how to live it meaningfully.

Benefits of Astrology

Astrology has a long and rich history, often used by our ancestors to guide daily decisions and bring clarity to the unknown. This science is still relevant today, offering many benefits to those who regularly practice it. Astrology can provide an understanding of ourselves and others by revealing past experiences, their potential for the future, and how certain factors may be influencing them in the present. It goes deeper than just star signs. Astrologers can assess planetary movements, explore zodiac birth charts, numerology cycles, and more to gain personal clarity and develop greater insight into people's lives. In addition, astrology teaches us valuable wisdom, including patience, as we wait for personal cycles to align with cosmic energies. By uncovering this ancient knowledge, you can make lasting improvements in your life and, perhaps most importantly, grow to accept your imperfections!

1. Understanding Personality

Astrology is an intriguing ancient practice that still resonates with many people today due to its striking accuracy. It can give you key insights into understanding yourself and your relationships with those around you. Through astrology, you can learn about your personality traits, helping you find the roots of why you think, speak, and behave the way you do. It can also shed light on how different personalities interact with each other, allowing you to create meaningful connections with others and cultivate better relationships. Besides providing valuable self-awareness, by regularly mapping out the movement of planets about your unique zodiac sign, astrology can also alert you to potential opportunities or dangers before they happen, putting you ahead of the game in terms of preparation and action. Regardless of the application, the advantages of utilizing astrology to understand yourself and others are abundantly clear.

2. Unlocking Life Lessons

Learning about astrology can be very beneficial in many ways. It can help you become more conscious of appropriate behavior, make you feel more connected to the Universe, and ultimately assist in your personal growth and development. Some may find it fascinating to learn that certain animals, planets, and symbols are associated with their life journey, expanding their knowledge beyond their present lives. Additionally, understanding where the stars stood at the time of birth provides powerful insights into how to interpret their influences on us. With research, practice, consultations, or classes, you can dive into your birth chart, unlocking valuable, insightful messages for guidance in your life. Accessing these life lessons from astrology provides you with guidance and a greater depth of insight that can help you live a happier and more meaningful life.

3. Gaining Insight into Life Situations

Unlocking the secrets of astrology can be a great tool for gaining insight into life situations and understanding your relationships with others. Although it's a complex study, some basics like star signs, compatibility charts, and even daily horoscopes are easy to understand. By taking the time to understand what is happening during any given time on the astrological calendar, you can learn more about yourself and gain valuable knowledge of events in your life. Whether predicting potential outcomes or giving advice on navigating tricky circumstances, astrology can be an invaluable resource in our journey of personal growth and self-awareness. With its help, you can discover everything from perfect timing to meaningful messages hidden within life events, truly understanding yourself and your interactions with those around you.

4. Strengthening Relationships

Strengthening relationships can be a challenge, but not impossible. Astrology is one tool people find useful to better understand themselves and their partners. It's a fun way to get to know your partner, or yourself, on a deeper level. From introducing some much-needed humor and understanding into conversations to uncovering previously unknown common interests, astrological readings open up pathways for communication between two people that wouldn't have been possible before. It shows you how your unique personality blends in ways you would never have imagined, allowing you to find new depths of connection with others in wonderful ways.

5. Discovering Talents and Strengths

Learning about astrology can be an excellent way to discover your talents and strengths. It can provide insight into your inner being, showing which qualities make you unique and which skills you already possess. By exploring the different signs and astrological principles, you may even find that some of your natural talents are unexpected or hidden beneath the surface. Additionally, understanding your strengths can make it easier to turn them into successful career paths or interests. Astrology also offers guidance on how to best use those gifts to explore new ideas, so you can make the most of them with a bit of determination.

6. Improving Time Management

Astrology is a powerful tool for improving time management. You know how hard it can be to juggle work, family life, hobbies, and personal health. With astrological guidance, however, you can start to organize the activities you need to do in the right sequence. A great benefit of understanding astrology is synchronizing activities to maximize results. This could mean doing tasks at the most suitable times each day or even designing your week around celestial rhythms that promote productivity. Astrology also refines your ability to prioritize tasks, allowing you to focus on your long-term goals while also addressing smaller tasks' importance. With improved time management skills through astrology, people can live a much more balanced and fulfilled life.

7. Promoting Spiritual Growth

Astrology is a great tool for promoting spiritual growth. It offers unique wisdom and insight into your life, personality, and relationships, all of which can help you become more aware of yourself and support your journey of self-discovery. By learning more about the stars, you can gain perspective on your current circumstances, release fear, and understand how to create the life you want. Whether it's getting clarity on an experience or discerning when might be the best time to take action on an important decision, astrology has the insight to guide you toward spiritual growth. With astrology, you can come to a greater understanding of who you are and why you behave in certain ways.

8. Improving Decision Making

Making choices and decisions can be difficult, especially when they have long-term implications. It's crucial to make the right decision, and here's where astrology can come in handy! Astrology is an incredible tool for improving decision-making, as it offers insight into your motivations, thoughts, and feelings. Additionally, it helps you gain perspective on your strengths and weaknesses and the possibilities when faced with a complex decision. By examining your astrological chart, you can gain clarity on your current situation and the consequences of certain decisions. Furthermore, astrology offers guidance toward making choices that are best aligned with your goals and desires, allowing you to make conscious decisions instead of blindly going through life without any insight or understanding of your core self. Ultimately, exploring astrological principles is an effective way to support yourself when making sound decisions and living healthier lives.

9. Discovering Purpose

Astrology can be a fascinating tool for self-discovery and ultimately fulfilling your purpose in life. With its 12 zodiac signs, astrology helps you to better understand yourself, including your strengths, weaknesses, and inclinations, which allows you to create the path that will bring you closer to your goals. By having an open mind and exploring the position of planets at various stages in your life, you can gain valuable insight into major life decisions like relationships, career moves, or educational pursuits. Believers see what they hope to be as symbols of their destiny in the placement of stars. Skeptics still have the chance to recognize meaning in their lives with knowledge derived from astrological study. Whether you think little or a lot about it, researching astrology may benefit you on your journey to discovering your purpose.

10. Moving Towards Fulfillment

In today's world of never-ending decisions, astrology can offer much-needed clarity. There are so many ways it can benefit your life, from uncovering personality traits and life paths to helping you to understand how you interact with certain people or develop relationships. With regular readings and advice tailored to a person's situation or planetary configuration, life decisions can become easier to make. Astrology is designed to provide guidance that ultimately allows room for improvement and growth toward fulfillment in all aspects of your life. Instead of dictating what you should do, it helps you reflect on where you are now, consider the future effects of any decision you may make, and figure out the best way forward for yourself in the long run. Instead of relying on luck or randomness to get you through rough patches in your life, astrology is a great option for finding your path toward true accomplishment and self-growth.

Interpreting an Astrological Chart

Interpreting an astrological chart can be a complex and bewildering process for the uninitiated. It requires knowledge of planetary interactions, sign representation, and symbolic language interpretation. The task may seem daunting, but it does not need to be. With practice and patience, interpreting astrological charts can become an enlightening tool to expand knowledge and understanding of the cyclical energy patterns in life. Start with smaller charts such as solar returns or daily transits to gain experience, and then progress onto more advanced charts as your confidence and abilities grow. Reach out to friends or online resources if you feel you need guidance. Never underestimate the support available to help you along your journey of unlocking the secrets within the stars.

A. Interactions between the Elements

Interpreting an astrological chart is an exciting and insightful way to appreciate the interactions between the elements. By studying the placement of planets in the zodiac and the relationships between them, it is possible to gain real insight into one's personality, connections with others, and potential outcomes. Astrology can be a great tool for self-reflection, allowing you to recognize your strengths and weaknesses and appreciate and understand another's perspective to have more meaningful interactions. With an accurate chart and interpretation of its contents, you can get to know yourself much more deeply than you ever thought possible.

B. Life Lessons and Personality Insight

Interpreting an astrological chart can be a great way to gain more insight into your life and personality. It's a practice that has been used for centuries, and people all around the world continue to use it today. The astrological chart is divided up into twelve houses, each representing different areas of your life such as home life, relationships, career, and more. Each house is connected to planetary placements and aspects that all influence each area. Because of this, examining an astrological chart can give you a better understanding of how those different elements in your life are all interconnected. Instead of just working on changing one isolated aspect of yourself, you can work on simultaneously improving many areas.

C. How to Interpret Charts in Depth

With the right tools and resources, you can delve into the different elements of a chart to paint a compelling picture of a person or situation. One great way to get started is to learn the language used in astrology to better understand the specific meanings behind each planet and sign. By combining this knowledge with expertise on transits and progressions, house placements, and aspects, individuals can slowly begin to unlock deeper layers of information hidden within their chart. There's so much to uncover when interpreting an astrological chart. With some dedication and practice, you'll soon feel confident interpreting yours!

Astrology readings can be incredibly informative and insightful, opening up avenues of possibilities in our lives. It has been around for centuries, and many people view it as an ancient art form. Interpreting astrological charts involves looking at the alignment of planets within a birth chart or a natal chart to gain insight into someone's essential character traits and life journey. The practice may seem obscure or esoteric, but understanding astrological meaning can help us uncover the hidden potential in ourselves and make sense of our destinies. With the right guide, tools, and resources, it is possible to gain a much deeper understanding of the mysteries of the stars. Dive right in and start deciphering your chart! Who knows what secrets you will uncover?

Chapter 2: Meet the Astrological Planets

Discovering the energy of the planets and how they can best interact with each astrological house is an exciting journey. All twelve houses have unique properties, so understanding various planetary influences on you can give you a genuinely fascinating insight into your life. The key to benefiting from the information that planets and astrology bring lies in learning the essential components of both fields and seeing which ones come together harmoniously. Learning about the planets' energies will be an invaluable tool for further discoveries.

The planets play an important role in astrology.
CactiStaccingCrane, CC BY-SA 4.0 <https://creativecommons.org/licenses/by-sa/4.0>, via Wikimedia Commons https://commons.wikimedia.org/wiki/File:Solar_System_true_color.jpg

This chapter will focus on the role of planets and explore each one in detail. The Sun, Moon, Mercury, Venus, Mars, Jupiter, Saturn, Uranus, Neptune, and Pluto will all be examined. The glyphs associated with each planet will be analyzed, as well as the keywords that best represent them, the deities they're associated with, the zodiac signs ruled by them, and the correspondences (elements, colors, crystals). Finally, a summary of the planet's energy and effects will be provided, so readers can get an idea of how the planet influences their life.

Understanding the Role of Planets in Astrology

Understanding the role of planets in astrology is a journey that can open your eyes to an entirely new way of looking at the world! As you begin to explore it, you'll discover how each planet symbolizes different qualities and meanings. The Sun, for example, governs the traits associated with one's conscious identity. Mercury is related to intellect and communication; Venus speaks to connection and harmony. Mars signifies energy and ambition. Saturn relates to responsibility and limitations. Jupiter speaks of abundance, growth, and expansiveness. Uranus represents shock, chaos, or a revolution in some aspects of life. Neptune suggests dreams and ephemerality, while Pluto pertains to transformation over time. By introducing yourself to the significance of planets in astrology, you can gain a fascinating insight into yourself as well as those around you on a much deeper level.

The Sun

The sun is a central figure in the study of astrology, providing you with illuminating insights into your character and behavior. It centers upon what is known as the Sun sign and is determined by where the sun was at the time of your birth. The Sun sign describes our natural dispositions and helps to define who we are. Used in combination with other astrological elements, it can also inform you about how you interact with others, your relationships, and what paths you should follow in life. Knowing your solar influence can be surprisingly helpful when making important decisions. Don't forget to look to the sky and find out what role the sun has to play in your life story!

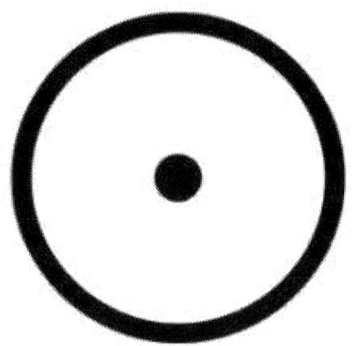

Sun glyph.
https://freesvg.org/sun-and-fish-ancient-symbol

A. Glyph Analysis

The glyph representing the sun is a circle with a dot in the center. This symbolizes how your life revolves around the power of this bright star, as it provides humans with energy and light. Additionally, the dot in the center of the circle suggests that within each person lies a special purpose or destiny.

B. Keywords

Powerful, light, inspiring, energizing, purposeful, illuminating

C. Associated Deities

Apollo, Ra, Helios, Amaterasu

D. Zodiac Sign(s) Ruled By It

Leo

E. Correspondences

- Element: Fire
- Color: Gold or Yellow
- Crystals: Citrine or Tiger's Eye
- Number: 1

F. Energy and Effects

The sun is a powerful symbol in astrology, representing the light and energy people receive from it. It can provide you with invaluable insights into your character and behavior. Furthermore, it can inform you of how you interact with others, your relationships, and what paths to follow in life. Knowing your solar influence can be a great help when making important decisions.

The Moon

The role of the Moon in astrology is fascinating and often overlooked. It is believed to be in charge of our energy, instincts, and emotions, and it also influences how people think and behave. When the Moon shifts position or enters a new sign, your way of processing the world changes with it due to its gravitational pull. According to astrologers, studying how the Moon moves through each zodiac sign can help you understand your subconscious responses and any extra intuition about certain topics or situations. Even though Astrology has been looked at with a lot of suspicions over the years, there is something soothing and reassuring about knowing that cosmic energies beyond your control can still positively affect you.

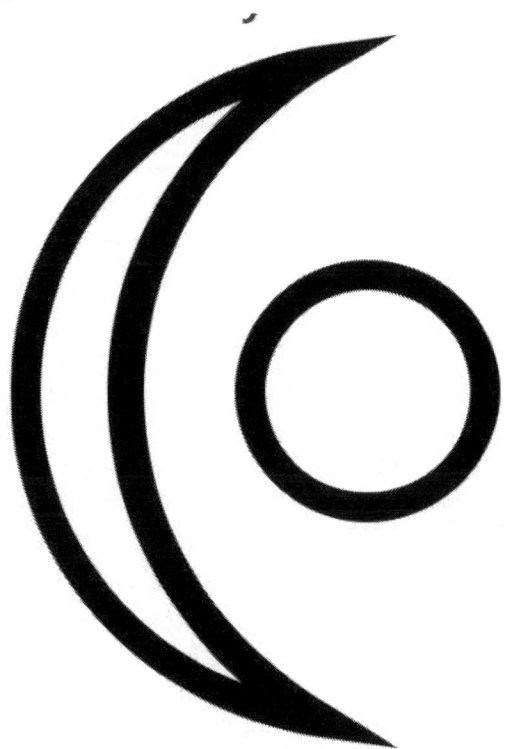

Moon glyph.
https://freesvg.org/illustration-of-a-symbol-with-crescent-shape-and-a-circle

A. Glyph Analysis

The glyph for the Moon is a crescent shape, reminding us of its connection with tides and natural cycles. It symbolizes your ability to adapt to changing circumstances and your capacity to be open and responsive to the ebb and flow of life.

B. Keywords

Intuition, emotions, energy, instincts, cycles

C. Associated Deities

Selene, Diana, Hecate

D. Zodiac Sign(s) Ruled By It

Cancer

E. Correspondences

- Element: Water
- Color: Silver or White
- Crystals: Moonstone or Aquamarine
- Number: 2

F. Energy and Effects

The Moon is an essential figure in astrology. Understanding its influence can provide us with valuable insight into our emotions, intuition, and instincts. The Moon's gravitational pull affects our ability to adapt to new situations. Its movements through the zodiac signs can guide you in your approach to life. Studying and learning about what this cosmic force offers can help you unlock your full potential and live life to the fullest. A more holistic understanding of cosmic energies in your life can make all the difference in making important decisions.

Mercury

The movements of Mercury are used to interpret a person's behavior, characteristics, and potential future. Mercury represents both logical thought and communication, and knowing this planet can give invaluable insights into how people think and express themselves. It is so influential that it reflects your decisions, values, and behavior as it relates to your relationships with others. Understanding the role of Mercury in astrology can be a powerful tool for understanding yourself and assisting you on your life path.

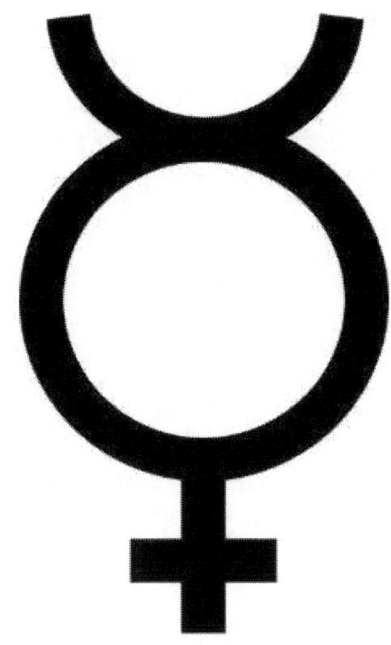

Mercury glyph.
https://www.needpix.com/photo/download/30682/planet-symbols-mercury-astronomical-planetary-astrological-astrology-free-vector-graphics-free-pictures

A. Glyph Analysis

The glyph for Mercury is a curve above a circle with a cross at the bottom, representing the duality that this planet stands for. It symbolizes your ability to think logically and effectively communicate with others.

B. Keywords

Communication, intelligence, logic, decisions, relationships

C. Associated Deities

Mercury, Hermes, Thoth

D. Zodiac Sign(s) Ruled By It

Gemini and Virgo

E. Correspondences

- Element: Air
- Color: Orange or Yellow
- Crystals: Citrine or Agate
- Number: 3

F. Energy and Effects

The movements of Mercury have a significant influence on how you think, behave, and communicate. Its duality is a reminder that your decisions and relationships with others must be balanced for you to live a fulfilling life. Taking the time to understand and learn the effects of Mercury can give you valuable insight into your own life and how you interact with others.

Venus

As astrology continues to draw in people from all walks of life, the role of Venus stands out as an especially interesting one. Named for the goddess of love and beauty, this planet is believed to govern the areas of love, relationships, and finances. Depending on a person's birth chart, the positioning of Venus can give great insight into an individual's character and destiny. More often than not, it guides them through difficult decisions in their personal lives as they strive to find a balance between their emotional needs and their practical obligations. Knowing more about Venus's influence on our lives can help us make more nuanced decisions that ultimately lead to greater happiness.

Venus glyph.
Font Awesome Free 5.2.0 by @fontawesome - https://fontawesome.com, CC BY 4.0
<https://creativecommons.org/licenses/by/4.0>, via Wikimedia Commons
https://upload.wikimedia.org/wikipedia/commons/6/66/Font_Awesome_5_solid_venus-mars.svg

A. Glyph Analysis

The glyph for Venus is a circle with a cross at the bottom, representing the feminine energy that this planet brings. It also has an element of balance, as the circle and cross represent a harmonious combination of mental and physical energies.

B. Keywords

Love, beauty, relationships, finances

C. Associated Deities

Venus, Aphrodite, Inanna

D. Zodiac Sign(s) Ruled By It

Taurus and Libra

E. Correspondences

- Element: Earth
- Color: Green or Pink
- Crystals: Rose Quartz or Jade
- Number: 6

F. Energy and Effects

Venus governs the areas of love, relationships, and finances. It helps you to find a balance between your emotional needs and practical responsibilities and to make informed decisions about the course your life should take. Understanding how Venus influences you can lead to more meaningful relationships and a greater sense of harmony in your life.

Mars

When it comes to astrology, the Red Planet Mars is incredibly influential as it has been studied for centuries. This celestial body plays an influential role in a person's zodiac chart and can be used to inform critical life decisions such as travel and career choices. Its energy can also symbolize drive, ambition, and passion, determining how active or determined someone may be. While its malefic aspects are associated with anger or aggression, its positive aspects can bring strength and courage into a person's life. Ultimately, understanding the effects of Mars in astrology can help a person tap into their true potential and take action.

Mars glyph.
IZN1TEN, CC BY-SA 4.0 <https://creativecommons.org/licenses/by-sa/4.0>, via Wikimedia Commons https://commons.wikimedia.org/wiki/File:Mars_symbol.jpg

A. Glyph Analysis

The glyph for Mars is a circle with an arrow, indicating the planet's aggressive nature. It is a symbol of strength and courage, which can be directed toward positive or negative outcomes.

B. Keywords

Action, aggression, ambition, passion

C. Associated Deities

Mars, Ares, Tyr

D. Zodiac Sign(s) Ruled By It

Aries and Scorpio

E. Correspondences

- Element: Fire
- Color: Red
- Crystals: Garnet or Bloodstone
- Number: 4

F. Energy and Effects

Mars is a powerful and influential planet in astrology, symbolizing drive, ambition, and passion. Taking the time to understand and learn about its effects can help people tap into their true potential and take action to achieve success. With this knowledge, individuals can become more aware of their energy and use it to manifest positive outcomes in all areas of life.

Jupiter

Jupiter is known as one of the most powerful and influential planets when it comes to astrology. Its role in the solar system goes beyond affecting people's lives. It's essential for the maintenance of a harmonious-balanced collective. When Jupiter goes retrograde, it creates an energetic barrier that deflects difficult energies that can affect your life in unfavorable ways. This acts like a screen that allows you to recognize when you are faced with external and internal challenges. Then, Jupiter acts as a life coach, encouraging you to look within to overcome your obstacles and strengthen your will by reinforcing your motivation. Additionally, because of Jupiter's expansive nature, it also helps increase energy production and general vitality. Therefore, Jupiter plays a major part in maintaining good luck and happiness!

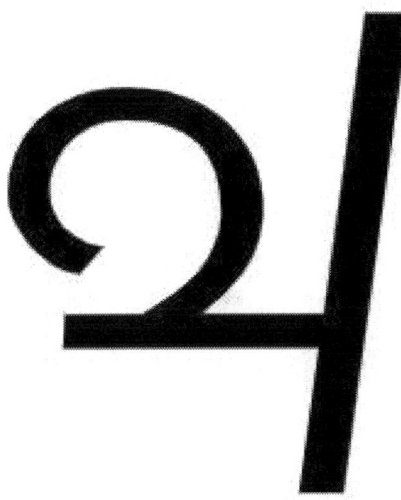

Jupiter glyph.
Creative Commons CC0 1.0 Universal Public Domain Dedication <
https://creativecommons.org/publicdomain/zero/1.0/deed.en>
https://upload.wikimedia.org/wikipedia/commons/5/5a/Rma_-_lh.svg

A. Glyph Analysis

The glyph for Jupiter combines two symbols, the crescent moon and the cross. This symbolizes life, growth, expansion, and spiritual and material abundance.

B. Keywords

Luck, expansion, happiness, growth

C. Associated Deities

Jupiter, Zeus, Odin

D. Zodiac Sign(s) Ruled By It

Sagittarius and Pisces

E. Correspondences

- Element: Fire
- Color: Purple or Blue
- Crystals: Amethyst or Lapis Lazuli
- Number: 3

F. Energy and Effects

Jupiter is an incredibly influential planet in astrology, symbolizing luck, expansion, happiness, and growth. Its energy can be beneficial when striving for success, and its retrograde periods can even help deflect negative energies. Jupiter encourages you to look within yourself to overcome obstacles and strengthen your will by reinforcing your motivation. Its expansive nature can help you increase your energy production and general vitality and bring more good luck to your life. Ultimately, understanding the effects of Jupiter in astrology can help a person tap into their true potential and achieve success.

Saturn

Saturn has a special place in astrology, for it rules over time and responsibility. It governs your experience in the physical world, helping you understand when to take action and prioritize tasks. Saturn also challenges you to strive for goals while teaching your soul lessons that force personal growth. Without Saturn's wisdom, you would be unable to move through life with courteous respect for natural law. This can lead to difficulty in experiencing success. With an understanding of the significance of Saturn in astrology, one can learn much about personal progress through timeless knowledge.

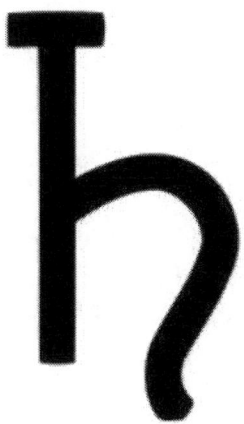

Saturn glyph.
Firkin CC0 1.0 Universal (CC0 1.0) Public Domain Dedication
https://creativecommons.org/publicdomain/zero/1.0/ https://openclipart.org/detail/227759/solar-system-symbols

A. Glyph Analysis

The glyph for Saturn is a cross with a curl at the bottom of it. This symbolizes duty, authority, and limitation, all of which come into play when Saturn is influencing us.

B. Keywords

Responsibility, structure, wisdom, law

C. Associated Deities

Saturn, Chronos, Shiva

D. Zodiac Sign(s) Ruled By It

Capricorn and Aquarius

E. Correspondences

- Element: Earth
- Color: Black or Gray
- Crystals: Jet or Hematite
- Number: 8

F. Energy and Effects

Saturn is an important planet in astrology, as it rules over time, responsibility, and authority. It teaches you to be mindful of your actions in life and how best to prioritize tasks. Saturn also encourages you to strive for success while teaching you valuable lessons that can help you grow and develop as an individual. When you understand the significance of Saturn in astrology, you can experience personal progress and benefit from timeless knowledge. With this, you can make conscious choices that bring you closer to your goals and create true success.

Uranus

Uranus is one of the most intriguing planets in astrology, known for its symbolism of rebellion, disruption, and liberation. Understanding Uranus' key role in any chart can provide valuable insight into a person's spiritual journey, and embracing the lessons associated with the planet can be a powerful source of transformation and growth. Placed within your unique natal birth chart, Uranus brings to light all aspects of your character which are non-conforming. It reveals how you express yourself differently from others and what unconventional paths you take in your life. Since Uranus rules over innovation, analyzing its placement in your astrological charts helps you understand where your creativity lies and drives you to make meaningful changes.

Uranus glyph.

A. Glyph Analysis

The glyph for Uranus is two half circles with a cross in the middle. This symbolizes movement, disruption, and liberation from restraints. The symbol contains a circle and cross-shaped elements that illustrate the planet's size and form, an interesting contrast to its colder temperature.

B. Keywords

Rebellion, disruption, liberation, creativity

C. Associated Deities

Uranus, Ea, Mithra

D. Zodiac Sign(s) Ruled By It

Aquarius

E. Correspondences

- Element: Air
- Color: Blue or Turquoise
- Crystals: Aquamarine or Tourmaline
- Number: 7

F. Energy and Effects

Uranus is one of the most interesting planets in astrology, known for its symbolism of rebellion, disruption, and liberation. Its placement in your astrological charts can help you understand your creative side and how to express yourself differently from others. Uranus teaches you to break free from restraints and embrace unconventional paths in life, which can lead to meaningful changes. With an understanding of the significance of Uranus in astrology, one can learn a lot about personal growth and transformation.

Neptune

Neptune is an intriguing planet within astrology, as it has been known to bring spiritual growth and higher consciousness. By understanding Neptune's role in astrology, you can use this knowledge to better understand yourself and your place in the universe. Specifically, Neptune's presence relates to your subconscious mind and its relation to dreams, creativity, and imagination. When you understand the power of Neptune, you can acknowledge that each person has access to the remarkable potential for spiritual transcendence and new understanding. Exploring Neptune's influence is a fascinating journey of self-discovery that may lead you to uncover hidden insights about yourself that have immense power for transformation!

Neptune glyph.
Firkin CC0 1.0 Universal (CC0 1.0) Public Domain Dedication
https://creativecommons.org/publicdomain/zero/1.0/ Solar system symbols - Openclipart

A. Glyph Analysis

The glyph for Neptune is a trident, an ancient symbol of authority and power. The trident also represents three prongs that represent the three aspects of Neptune, including spirituality, creativity, and imagination.

B. Keywords

Mysterious, spiritual, creative, imaginative

C. Associated Deities

Neptune, Poseidon, Manannan Mac Lir

D. Zodiac Sign(s) Ruled By It

Pisces

E. Correspondences

- Element: Water
- Color: Blue or Purple
- Crystals: Moonstone or Amethyst
- Number: 8

F. Energy and Effects

Neptune is astrology's powerful and mysterious planet, often associated with spiritual growth and higher consciousness. Analyzing Neptune's role in your astrological chart can help you to understand your subconscious mind and its influence on your dreams, creativity, and imagination. By understanding Neptune's significance in astrology, you can access tremendous potential for spiritual transcendence and unlock new insights about yourself that can transform your life.

Pluto

As a small, distant planet in Earth's solar system, Pluto has often been overlooked in astrology. However, that's no longer the case. As an outer planet, Pluto can have a strong influence on you. It often signifies transformation and momentous life changes. Astrological interpretations suggest that Pluto represents one's ability to dig deep into their truth and innermost desires. By understanding Pluto's symbolism, you can gain insight into your maturity. The energy of this planet can guide powerful discoveries within ourselves, from breaking old habits and misconceptions to embracing who we truly are.

Pluto glyph.

A. Glyph Analysis

The glyph for Pluto is a small circle with a cross underneath it, symbolizing the planet's deep and mysterious nature. The circle represents unity, while the cross suggests transformation, composed of two intersecting lines representing different directions.

B. Keywords

Mysterious, transformative, powerful, intense

C. Associated Deities

Pluto, Demeter, Hades

D. Zodiac Sign(s) Ruled by It

Scorpio

E. Correspondences

- Element: Water
- Color: Black
- Crystals: Obsidian or Jet
- Number: 8

F. Energy and Effects

Pluto is a small, distant planet in the solar system that often signifies transformation and momentous life changes. By understanding Pluto's symbolism, you can gain insight into your maturity. Exploring the energy of this planet can guide powerful discoveries within yourself and can help you to break old habits and misconceptions and embrace who you truly are.

In conclusion, the planets (Sun, Moon, Mercury, Venus, Mars, Jupiter, Saturn, Uranus, Neptune, and Pluto) of astrology each have their special energy and influence the lives of individuals in unique ways. By exploring these planets, you can gain valuable insight into your personal growth and development. By understanding each planet's symbolism, you can unlock hidden truths about yourself and use that knowledge to create meaningful change in your life.

Chapter 3: Nodes and Asteroids Matter, Too

The core mechanics of astrology can often be drilled down to the influence of the planets. They shine a light on personality traits, relational interactions, and much more. While these celestial bodies are majorly responsible for defining the energies that shape you astrologically, there are minor energies that shouldn't be overlooked. Asteroids and nodes complete an intricate cosmic puzzle that helps you to fully understand yourself. The asteroids often depict your innermost emotions and relationships, while the nodes provide hidden influences or behaviors that are still impactful.

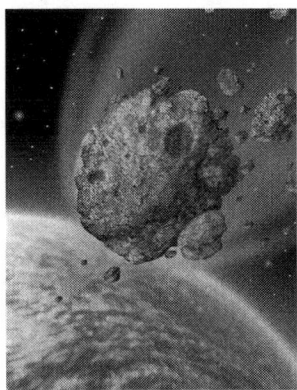

Asteroids play a role in astrological readings.
State Farm, CC BY 2.0 <https://creativecommons.org/licenses/by/2.0>, via Wikimedia Commons
https://commons.wikimedia.org/wiki/File:Asteroid_falling_to_Earth.jpg

Astrology relies on major and minor energies to gain a clear picture of your life or even past lives that you can look into for deeper understanding. These energies come together to create something personal, an in-depth reading that provides insight into who you are and what potential paths exist in front of you. It's an interesting way to reflect on ourselves and find solace in discovering the unique beauty that comes from your cosmic origins.

This chapter will explore two of astrology's most important minor energies, including asteroids and the nodes. It will break down their meanings and roles in your life, explain how they can affect you, what lessons they teach, and how they work together to create a complete picture of your life. By the end of this chapter, you will better understand the importance of minor energies in astrology and how they can be used to help you make better decisions.

Nodes

Astrology can be an interesting and complex field to study. In astrology, Nodes refer to the North and South Node, which represent your Karmic past and where your soul is heading. By determining the location of the Nodes in our birth chart, one can learn more about their past life influences and their place in their current journey. Studying nodes in astrology can shed light on how we're creating or manifesting certain aspects of our life, so it can be a great learning tool for anyone looking to gain a deeper understanding of their own lives. Also, exploring astrological nodes helps you learn more about why you are drawn to some people and repelled by others or why some situations attract you while others turn you off. Overall, it's a great exercise in self-discovery, and there is so much to discover!

A. Definition of Nodes

The nodes in astrology are two very specific points on the celestial sphere representing a philosophical clash between one's past, present, and future. The north node represents the most beneficial path for you to follow, and the south node represents lessons from your experiences. They are not planets or signs. They are mathematical points that provide insight into your life to maximize your potential and better understand your dilemmas and challenges. Every cycle of the nodes around the chart takes roughly eighteen months, making it an incredibly powerful tool when studying personal growth and collective shifts. Of course, astrology is not limited to just these two points. Still, it can provide you with incredible insight into your spiritual and material pursuits.

B. South Node

Have you ever heard of the South Node in Astrology? This critical concept is about looking into your past and unpacking how past experiences shape you today. The South Node relates to where you come from on your spiritual journeys, and it speaks to who you were before this current life. As the astrological sign closest to the body's energy field, the South Node can tell you about previous karmic patterns, such as beliefs, feelings, and expectations that may be holding you back from achieving future goals. It is truly an intriguing concept that is well worth exploring if you want to understand yourself or those around you on a deeper level.

C. North Node

Understanding your North Node in astrology can be a fascinating journey. It requires looking back at the past, delving into your story, and coming up with a fresh perspective. Your North Node is believed to be connected to your destiny and the highest realization of yourself. Consider this equivalent to your zodiac's version of a flight plan. Understanding it could provide invaluable insight into who you are and where you're headed. It could also help with making difficult decisions on what new beginnings will align with your higher purpose. Take some time for deeper exploration and reflect on how your North Node lessons might help you find more joy and fulfillment in life.

D. Role of Black Moon Lilith

In the world of Astrology, Black Moon Lilith is an incredibly influential figure. This mysterious object can reveal vital insights into your life and your relationships with others, including its effects on you both individually and collectively. Lilith represents the more shadowy sides of your soul, such as dark energy, self-sabotage, self-destructive behaviors, repressed desires, and even trauma that has been left unresolved. But it can also point to your capacity for transformative growth and strength. Taking the time to understand your own Black Moon Lilith opens up a whole new realm of possibilities for personal insight, healing, and growth in life.

Asteroids

For many people, asteroids can be fascinating petite planets that provide enigmatic messages about our destinies. They play an essential role in astrology, as the individual patterns formed by the configuration of asteroids in your chart reveal hidden insights. Looking at asteroid astrology provides a roadmap to understanding certain events and behaviors in your life. Every placement lets you delve deeper into who you are and where you are heading. From Juno revealing where commitment comes from to Chiron connecting us to past soul wounds and Ceres helping you find patterns within both positive and negative experiences, asteroids give you intricate knowledge about life's many mysteries.

Chiron

The mighty asteroid of Chiron has long been a source of interest for astrologers. Commonly known as the "wounded healer" due to its unpredictable and paradoxical nature, it is believed to represent your capacity for compassion and understanding. This asteroid helps you understand your life's purpose and thus better plan for your life moving forward. It also has great symbolic meaning in terms of showing how you can rise above the suffering in your life, regardless of its form or intensity. As such, astrologers often look towards this ancient celestial body when interpreting the stars and gaining insight into your experiences. With its unique interpretation, Chiron is truly a special asteroid with deep connections within astrology.

A. Glyph Analysis

After analyzing its glyph, it appears that the "C" shape indicates energy circulation within the solar system, while the two main lines represent the sun-earth relationship. The glyph also includes a symbol pointing toward our place in this phenomenon. This symbolic representation teaches you to be aware of your role as a part of a much bigger systemic structure and reminds you to be mindful of how you interact with it.

B. Keywords

Transformation, growth, healing

C. Associated Deities

Apollo, Artemis, Hecate, Prometheus, Hygeia

D. Zodiac Sign(s) Ruled By It
Aries, Leo, Sagittarius

E. Correspondences
- Element: Fire
- Color: Gold
- Crystals: Amethyst, Moonstone
- Number: 9

F. Energy and Effects

Chiron is an asteroid associated with transformation, growth, healing, and understanding. It has a powerful impact on the energy of those it influences and empowers them to make changes in their lives. It can offer insight into the purpose of suffering and how your wounds can be used to create something beautiful. By connecting to its energy, you can better understand your destinies and find the strength to overcome any obstacles. Ultimately, Chiron reminds you to let go of the past, embrace your wounds, and use them to keep growing.

Ceres

What is the astrological significance of the dwarf planet Ceres? This is a question that has been asked by many throughout history. It turns out that this asteroid has an important role to play in the cosmos, with particular relevance for individuals who follow astrology. From its place within the solar system, Ceres is thought to influence your life and contribute to a balance between your nature, growth, and nourishment. Studying this asteroid can give you greater insight into yourself and your purpose here on Earth. For those interested in taking a deeper look, researching how our relationship with this celestial body influences our relationships with others can be enlightening.

A. Glyph Analysis

The glyph of Ceres is composed of two circles, with a cross in the center, representing fertility and nourishment. The circles represent the earth, while the cross in the center suggests that all living things are connected. This glyph is also symbolic of Ceres' role as a guardian and caretaker of the Earth by providing sustenance to all living things.

B. Keywords

Abundance, nurture, fertility, motherhood

C. Associated Deities

Demeter, Aphrodite, Persephone, Cybele

D. Zodiac Sign(s) Ruled By It

Taurus, Virgo, Capricorn

E. Correspondences

- Element: Earth
- Color: Green
- Crystals: Chrysoprase, Jade
- Number: 5

F. Energy and Effects

Ceres is an asteroid associated with abundance, nurture, fertility, and motherhood. It is believed to strongly influence your relationships with other people and your environment. By connecting to its energy, you can better understand your identity and purpose in life. It encourages you to be more nurturing, compassionate, and generous toward yourself and those around you. Ultimately, Ceres reminds you to take care of yourself and those close to you, so you can be the best version of yourself.

Pallas

Astrologers have long been intrigued by the mysterious Pallas asteroid because of its close relationship with your innermost thoughts as it relates to self-mastery and wisdom. Symbolically, this asteroid carries metaphysical insight into how you act in the world. It is believed that understanding your directive, purpose, and motivation can help you grow spiritually and even break old patterns of behavior which impede your progress. Although the Pallas asteroid speaks mostly to the deeper spiritual aspects within everyone, it also speaks to the outer environment since several myths include it as a symbol of protection against enemies, both hidden and obvious. Finally, because of its connection to wisdom, astrologers often look to its insights when trying to unravel tough life issues such as relationships or career decisions.

A. Glyph Analysis

The glyph of Pallas is composed of a shield and spear, representing protection and strength. It suggests that Pallas plays an essential role in guarding people against their enemies by providing them with the wisdom and bravery to overcome obstacles.

B. Keywords

Protection, strength, wisdom, strategy

C. Associated Deities

Athena, Minerva, Nike

D. Zodiac Sign(s) Ruled By It

Aquarius, Libra

E. Correspondences

- Element: Air
- Color: Silver
- Crystals: Hematite, Jet
- Number: 8

F. Energy and Effects

Pallas is an asteroid that helps you be mindful of how you act and understand your role. Its energy can give you strength, courage, and confidence to take on the challenges that come your way and make decisions with clarity and purpose. By connecting to its energy, you can gain greater insight into your life's direction and increase your chances of success in your endeavors. Pallas reminds you to trust yourself and step out of your comfort zone to reach your highest potential. It encourages you to use strategy and wisdom to protect yourself against any kind of external or internal enemies.

Juno

Juno is an asteroid that has been coming into focus lately, particularly due to its relation to astrology. Named for the Roman goddess of marriage and romance, Juno is seen as a significant symbol amongst stargazers, carrying messages of partnership and devotion. Astrologers across the globe have attributed different meanings to it, from exploring heartbreak, and honoring female principles, to creating profound unions with other individuals (relationships that result in stability and delight). Its discovery adds insight into the many mysteries of the skies, thought-provoking and captivating. The sight of Juno in a person's natal chart may excite or spark caution, depending on how it's perceived, leading you to look deeper into how love shows up in your life.

A. Glyph Analysis

The glyph of Juno is a triangular shape, with two open and one closed side. This signifies the mixed bag of emotions that come along with love and relationships, showing the balance between openness and protection when it comes to partnership.

B. Keywords

Love, marriage, commitment, union, relationship

C. Associated Deities

Juno, Venus

D. Zodiac Sign(s) Ruled By It

Taurus, Libra

E. Correspondences

- Element: Earth
- Color: Red and Pink
- Crystals: Rose Quartz, Rhodonite
- Number: 6

F. Energy and Effects

Juno's energy encourages you to explore how to approach relationships and find joy and fulfillment in your partnerships. It can create an awareness of the importance of commitment, responsibility, and trust in any relationship dynamic. Juno's energy can allow you to create deeper connections with those closest to you and encourages you to operate from a place of love instead of fear. It teaches you to take a stand for your own needs while still allowing you to be open and vulnerable. Juno encourages you to focus on the basic needs of partnership and to find strength in your relationship bonds. By connecting with its energy, you can create an atmosphere of mutual respect and understanding, allowing you to create loving and lasting unions.

Vesta

Astrology enthusiasts have a new source of fascination in the Vesta asteroid, considered to be the brightest object in the asteroid belt. Discovered by German astronomer Heinrich Olbers in 1807, it is thought to represent Virgo, the Virgin Maiden of ancient goddess myths. Those who think your destiny is written in the stars believe Vesta's influence could bring clarity and help achieve goals with minimal effort. Other astrological interpretations suggest that it can enhance sexual relationships, family life, and feelings of camaraderie. Regardless of what path you choose to explore or how you interpret Vesta's influence on your life, its magnetism will surely take you on an interesting journey!

A. Glyph Analysis

The glyph for Vesta is two intersecting circles, representing the union of spiritual and physical energies. It also symbolizes the combination of material and spiritual gifts that we, as individuals, can use to reach our highest potential.

B. Keywords

Focused, dedicated, devoted, passionate, disciplined

C. Associated Deities

Vesta, Hestia, Athena

D. Zodiac Sign(s) Ruled By It

Virgo

E. Correspondences

- Element: Earth
- Color: White and Silver
- Crystals: Rock Crystal, Obsidian
- Number: 5

F. Energy and Effects

Vesta's energy encourages you to remain devoted and passionate about what matters most to you. It helps you to stay focused and remember the importance of your dedication, even when faced with obstacles or setbacks. This energy can inspire feelings of security and trust within relationships and a sense of camaraderie or "team spirit." Vesta can help you stay devoted to your goals, dreams, and ambitions in life. Its energy can also bring a sense of balance and harmony to any situation, allowing you to stay true to yourself and your values. When you tap into the power of Vesta, you can remain disciplined and passionate about your pursuits while still being gentle and understanding toward others.

Eros

Astronomers worldwide are highly familiar with Eros Asteroid, a celestial body renowned for its cosmic significance. It is believed to influence individuals based on their birth date, helping to provide a glimpse at what can be expected in their lives. This very special celestial body interacts with the most personal parts of our natal chart and transmits amazing energy that can help you to soar or falter, depending on how it's activated. Astrologers look at the many aspects of Eros Asteroid to gain insights into what's happening both inside and outside an individual. From facing forces within yourself, understanding your desires, improving communication skills, and finding the right kind of love, Eros has a mix of various elements that make it truly unique. Its effects feel like nothing else, providing you with a powerful force to explore yourself more deeply.

A. Glyph Analysis

The glyph for Eros is a circle with an arrow pointing downward. This symbolizes the powerful and passionate energy of love and the ability to penetrate and open up what had previously been closed off.

B. Keywords

Romance, passion, intimacy, desire, sensuality

C. Associated Deities

Eros, Aphrodite, Cupid

D. Zodiac Sign(s) Ruled By It

Taurus, Libra

E. Correspondences

- Element: Water
- Color: Red and Pink
- Crystals: Rose Quartz, Garnet
- Number: 7

F. Energy and Effects

Eros is the god of love, passion, and intimacy. His energy helps you open your heart and find the courage to express yourself authentically in relationships. It encourages you to take risks and embrace your desires while giving you the courage to explore new avenues. This energy can help you access a deeper connection with yourself and others, allowing you to break free from your inhibitions and discover a passion for life. Eros also helps you open up to the healing power of love and experience the joys of intimate relationships. With his energy, you can deepen your understanding of yourself and others and find the courage to take risks and explore your passions.

Hygeia

Hygeia, or asteroid 10, is one of the largest asteroids in the Solar System and has been thought to have a powerful influence on astrology. Named after the Greek goddess of health, Hygeia was discovered in 1854 and has since become a powerhouse for understanding our psychological nature. People look into their natal chart right around the placement of Hygeia to find greater clarity about health issues that could be affecting their life journey and how they can better care for themselves. The asteroid symbolizes prevention, healthy boundaries, and good habits, so it can help people take back control over their well-being. Plus, with all its links to mystical forces that are beyond our understanding, learning more about Hygeia can be quite an adventure.

A. Glyph Analysis

The glyph for Hygeia is a bowl with a serpent wrapped around it. This symbolizes the protection, healing, and nourishment that Hygeia can provide. It also represents the need for boundaries and limits in life, as well as our ability to take care of ourselves in a holistic way.

B. Keywords

Health, self-care, protection, boundaries, limits

C. Associated Deities

Hygeia, Asclepius

D. Zodiac Sign(s) Ruled By It

Virgo

E. Correspondences
- Element: Earth
- Color: Green and Yellow
- Crystals: Jade, Chrysocolla, Tiger's Eye
- Number: 9

F. Energy and Effects

Hygeia's energy encourages us to care for our physical and emotional health by setting boundaries and limits. It helps you find healing in your body, mind, and spirit and teaches you to look after yourself holistically. This energy also emphasizes the importance of understanding your limits and having the courage to set them to be able to enjoy a healthy lifestyle. Hygeia's energy encourages you to be vigilant in your self-care and preventative health while helping you recognize your need for boundaries. Finally, this energy teaches you to listen to your body and respect its warnings to stay healthy. Hygeia's energy helps you become more knowledgeable and aware of your well-being, making your best choices.

Astrology is an incredible science for interpreting the subtle messages of the zodiac and gaining insight into your life. Two significant sources astrologers use to understand the stars are asteroids and nodes. Asteroids offer a detailed interpretation of your relationship with others and your world, while nodes signify important turning points in your life journey. Together, these cosmic elements bring a deeper perspective to the meanings behind your zodiac sign. Studying these powerful tools can be incredibly rewarding as you explore the often mysterious language of the cosmos.

Chapter 4: The 12 Zodiac Signs

Zodiac signs allow you to glimpse the magnificence of the cosmos by providing insight into how the energy of planets, asteroids, and nodes in the solar systems affect people. Each sign corresponds with its unique influences, affecting different areas of your life, such as your personality, relationships, and lifestyle choices. By learning the different traits associated with each sign, you can learn more about yourself and apply this information to make better decisions for living a fulfilling life. Consulting astrological forecasts based on your zodiac sign can unlock greater wisdom and understanding that you never knew existed. It's like opening the door to an entirely new perspective.

The zodiac wheel.
DG-RA CC0 1.0 Universal (CC0 1.0) Public Domain Dedication,
https://creativecommons.org/publicdomain/zero/1.0/ https://openclipart.org/detail/307964/signs-of-the-zodiacs

This chapter will explore the significance of each sign in depth. Starting with a brief overview of the wheel of zodiac signs, it will then delve into examining each sign in detail, from the meaning behind its glyph and symbol through to the introduction of its ruling planet, as well as other correspondences (such as color, metal, stone, and body part). By the end of this chapter, you will have a better idea of what each sign brings to the table and how it shapes your life and character.

Whether you believe in astrology or not, there's a fascinating beauty to the wheel of stars and planets that spells out a possible destiny from birth. Each sign has its characteristics and traits associated with it, ranging from the bubbly Aries to the responsible Capricorn. At this wheel of fate, you can get to know yourself better, find those around you easier to understand, jumpstart your creativity, and even achieve a more peaceful temperament. It won't give you exact answers, but it will help you make better choices on your journey through life.

A Closer Look at Each Sign

Learning about the different zodiac signs can be incredibly enlightening and surprisingly accurate! Zodiac signs are based on the Earth's cycles, as seen through classical astrology. They aim to provide insight into your personality, motivation, and interactions with others. Begin by familiarizing yourself with each zodiac sign's unique characteristics, from Aries' adventurousness to Pisces' sensitivity. You can then explore your sign's compatibility with others or dive deeper into how each interacts differently with relationships, career paths, and more. Get ready to explore this fascinating world. Who knows what you will find out about yourself?

Aries (March 21–April 19)

Those born between March 21 and April 19 will most likely have a fiery temper and an eager attitude to match their Zodiac sign, Aries. No task is too challenging for this determined sign, which also means that Aries natives usually don't take no for an answer. They'll rightly focus their incredible energy on what makes them truly passionate. They also remain level-headed when it comes to anything else. An Aries will often take the initiative in matters where others lack motivation or are unwilling to take action. If you're looking for someone who won't back down and can give it their all in any situation, then an Aries might just be the perfect fit.

A. Glyph and Symbol

The glyph of Aries is that of a ram's horns, while the symbol is a ram itself. Both represent the sign's determination and willingness to go above and beyond for success. This can describe their unwavering nature and the courage and determination they exhibit when faced with a challenge.

B. Keywords

Courageous, Energetic, Determined

C. Element

Aries is a Fire sign, and its element is Fire, which represents passion and enthusiasm. This zodiac sign is all about action and taking the initiative, which explains why they often seem unstoppable.

D. Modality

Aries is a cardinal sign, meaning they usually lead with enthusiasm and eagerness to try new things. They are not afraid of taking risks or being the first to take a leap of faith.

E. Planet

Mars is the ruling planet of Aries, and its influence can be seen in the native's fiery temper and strong-willed nature.

F. Polarity

Aries is a positive sign, meaning they tend to be optimistic, focused, and determined in their approach.

G. Correspondences

- Color: Red
- Metal: Iron
- Stone: Diamond
- Body Part: Head and face.

Taurus (April 20–May 20)

The Taurus sign is associated with stability, firmness, and dependability, essential traits in life's most important relationships. Ruled by Venus, the planet of beauty and love, these zodiac lovers prefer comfort and security in all their endeavors. The earth element of Taurus gives them an affinity for nature, which often leads to a penchant for home comforts and a slow-paced lifestyle. They like their lives to move at a leisurely pace, allowing them sufficient time to enjoy the finer things in life. Those born under this star sign possess great perseverance and determination, with strong intuitions to guide their decisions. Sensual by nature, Taurus is romantic, devoted, and faithful, which makes them fantastic friends and partners.

A. Glyph and Symbol

The glyph of Taurus is the bull's head, while its symbol is a bull. These represent the sign's strong will and determination, as well as its loyalty to loved ones and its tendency to remain steadfast.

B. Keywords

Stable, Dependable, Loyal

C. Element

Taurus is an Earth sign, and its element is Earth which symbolizes stability and reliability. This zodiac sign is all about slow-paced stability, preferring to take their time when making decisions.

D. Modality

Taurus is a fixed sign, meaning they are focused and determined to stay true to their goals and values. They have unshakable confidence in their convictions and won't waver even when faced with adversity.

E. Planet

Venus is the ruling planet of Taurus, and its influence can be seen in the sign's appreciation for beauty and love. They tend to be romantic, devoted, and faithful, making them fantastic friends and companions.

F. Polarity

Taurus is a positive sign, meaning they tend to be optimistic and focused on their goals. They have a strong will and determination that allow them to stay true to their convictions no matter what.

G. Correspondences

- Color: Green
- Metal: Copper
- Stone: Emerald
- Body Part: Throat and neck.

Gemini (May 21–June 21)

Gemini is the ultimate chameleon. Changeable and versatile, they can fit in with any group of people regardless of their background. Gemini people are born to communicate, often speaking with a natural flair that is sure to captivate those around them. They have encyclopedic knowledge stored up in their head, so don't be surprised if you find yourself getting lost in conversation with one. Their open-mindedness and curiosity drive them to learn more about the world and seek out stimulating new experiences. All these things come together to make Geminis truly rewarding friends who are sure to bring plenty of joy into your life.

A. Glyph and Symbol

The glyph of Gemini is two crescent moons, while its symbol is the twins. This symbolizes the sign's dual nature and its ability to adapt to any situation.

B. Keywords

Adaptable, Versatile, Intelligent

C. Element

Gemini is an Air sign that symbolizes the sign's need for intellectual stimulation and the ability to think quickly. It is associated with communication, ideas, and creativity.

D. Modality

Gemini is a Mutable sign, which means it is flexible and open to change. They have a knack for adapting to any situation and can easily switch between different tasks.

E. Planet

Mercury is the ruling planet of Gemini. Its influence can be seen in the sign's keen intellect and excellent communication skills.

F. Polarity

Gemini is a positive sign, meaning that they are optimistic and open-minded. They can easily adapt to any situation, and their enthusiasm and energy can bring plenty of joy into your life.

G. Correspondences
- Color: Yellow
- Metal: Mercury
- Stone: Agate
- Body Part: Arms and hands.

Cancer (June 22–July 22)

The Cancer zodiac sign is known for its compassion and thoughtfulness. People born under the Cancer sign are often considered to be intuitive with a great capacity for understanding others. They strive to make everyone around them feel secure and emotionally cared for. These qualities, combined with their strong survival skills, make them an asset in any team project. In relationships, Cancers tend to be loyal, devoted, and protective of those they love. Although they may become moody or reclusive at times, they demonstrate incredible strength and resilience regarding life's biggest challenges.

A. Glyph and Symbol

The glyph of Cancer is the crab, while its symbol is the Crab's claw. This symbolizes the sign's ability to protect and nurture those it loves.

B. Keywords

Loyal, Nurturing, Protective

C. Element

Cancer is a Water sign that symbolizes the sign's strong emotional nature and the need for security and stability. It is associated with empathy, sensitivity, and intuition.

D. Modality

Cancer is a Cardinal sign which means that the sign is driven and goal-oriented. They are motivated to take the initiative and get things done, no matter the challenge.

E. Planet

The Moon is the ruling planet of Cancer. Its influence can be seen in the sign's strong emotional nature and need for security.

F. Polarity

Cancer is a negative sign, meaning that they are introspective and empathetic. They are devoted to their loved ones and strive to create a safe and secure environment for them.

G. Correspondences

- Color: Silver
- Metal: Moon
- Stone: Moonstone
- Body Part: Chest and stomach.

Leo (July 23–August 22)

Leo is a fire sign, which means its symbolization is greatly inspired by the sun. Leos strive for success and energy, aiming to be noticed and recognized. People under this sign are born with leadership traits that allow them to succeed in almost any path they choose in life. They are always willing to try something new, always looking for something that fulfills their need for creativity. This is an inspiring sign of persistence and courage that never fails to draw the attention of others. Generally speaking, Leos will always stand out from the crowd because of their generous nature and positive attitude. No wonder it's considered one of the strongest zodiac signs around.

A. Glyph and Symbol

The glyph of Leo is the Lion, while its symbol is a lion's head. This symbolizes the sign's strong nature, as well as its leadership traits.

B. Keywords

Generous, Energetic, Confident

C. Element

Leo is a Fire sign symbolizing the sign's strong will and passion. It is associated with strength, enthusiasm, and creativity.

D. Modality

Leo is a fixed sign which means that the sign is reliable, focused, and hard-working. They are determined to finish what they start and never give up on their goals.

E. Planet

The Sun is the ruling planet of Leo, and its influence can be seen in the sign's strong drive and ambition.

F. Polarity

Leo is a positive sign, meaning that they are confident and passionate. They are generous and optimistic, always striving to improve the world.

G. Correspondences

- Color: Gold
- Metal: Sun
- Stone: Ruby
- Body Part: Heart and spine.

Virgo (August 23–September 22)

If you're born between August 23 and September 22, then you are a Virgo. Virgos tend to be very analytical and detail-oriented, making great executives or problem solvers. They also value ethics and treat others with respect. It is not uncommon for them to dream big but take measured steps to reach their goals. Their organizational skills mean that they excel at anything requiring precision and attention to detail, while their perception helps them understand the workings of the world around them. Although they may come across as perfectionists, deep down, they are generally compassionate souls who deeply care about lifestyle improvement and the welfare of their close friends and family. Overall, having a Virgo in your life is a rewarding experience. You'll have a loyal friend for life if you earn their trust.

A. Glyph and Symbol

The glyph of Virgo is the Maiden, while its symbol is a Virgin woman. This symbolizes the sign's purity and innocence.

B. Keywords

Analytical, Detail-oriented, Ethical

C. Element

Virgo is an Earth sign which symbolizes the sign's practicality and stability. It is associated with structure, grounding, and productivity.

D. Modality

Virgo is a Mutable sign which means that the sign is adaptable, flexible, and open-minded. They can easily take on new tasks and change directions if needed.

E. Planet

The ruling planet of Virgo is Mercury, and its influence can be seen in the sign's analytical mind and love of communication.

F. Polarity

Virgo is a Negative sign, meaning they tend to be more introverted and concerned with the details. They are focused on improving themselves rather than relying on external sources.

G. Correspondences

- Color: Silver
- Metal: Mercury
- Stone: Peridot
- Body Part: Intestinal system.

Libra (September 23–October 23)

Libra is an air sign, which means creativity and intellectual curiosity are at the core of their being. People born under the Libra zodiac sign have an innate sense of balance and harmony, making them great problem-solvers and peacemakers. They are strikingly social creatures whose charm puts people at ease, friends, acquaintances, and strangers alike because they can always see different sides of complex situations or problems. Whether they can easily organize parties or just have a good time, Libras are sure to make any event more enjoyable. Ultimately, nothing matters more to this sign than finding balance in all areas of life, including work, play, and relationships.

A. Glyph and Symbol

The glyph of Libra is the Scales, while its symbol is a pair of scales balanced between two horizontal lines. This symbolizes the sign's search for balance and justice in all aspects of life.

B. Keywords

Social, Harmonious, Balanced

C. Element

Libra is an Air sign which symbolizes the sign's intellectual curiosity and creativity. It is associated with communication, knowledge, and connecting ideas.

D. Modality

Libra is a Cardinal sign which means that the sign is a natural leader who can take charge and motivate others. They are driven to succeed, but their sense of justice prevents them from taking shortcuts.

E. Planet

The ruling planet of Libra is Venus, and its influence can be seen in the sign's charm and beauty.

F. Polarity

Libra is a Positive sign, meaning that they naturally strive for harmony in all areas of life. They are focused on connecting with others instead of relying on internal sources.

G. Correspondences

- Color: Pastel Blue
- Metal: Copper
- Stone: Opal
- Body Part: Lower Back.

Scorpio (October 24–November 21)

Scorpios are known for being passionate, intense, and intuitive people. These qualities make them great leaders. Those born under Scorpio live life with a strong sense of power and purpose. This can manifest in their deep insights and understanding, often seeing into the heart of a problem or situation more quickly than others. They also have an unyielding determination for success coupled with an uncanny ability to adapt through challenging times that helps them reach their goals. With this combination of qualities, it should be no surprise that they often find themselves leaders in most of their chosen endeavors. If you know someone born under this star sign, be sure to appreciate them and all they bring to the table.

A. Glyph and Symbol

The glyph of Scorpio is a Scorpion with its tail pointing downward, symbolizing the sign's ability to strike with precision and accuracy. Its symbol is the same.

B. Keywords

Powerful, Intense, Adaptable

C. Element

Scorpio is a Water sign which symbolizes their strong intuition and emotional depth. It is associated with feelings, emotions, and the collective unconscious.

D. Modality

Scorpio is a fixed sign which means that the sign is focused on finding strength and stability in their lives. They are loyal to those they love and tenacious in their pursuits, never giving up until they find their desired outcome.

E. Planet

The ruling planet of Scorpio is Mars, and its influence can be seen in the sign's courage and determination.

F. Polarity

Scorpio is a Negative sign, meaning they are more focused on internal sources of power than external ones.

G. Correspondences

- Color: Dark Red
- Metal: Steel
- Stone: Topaz
- Body Part: Reproductive Organs.

Sagittarius (November 22–December 21)

Sagittarians are known for having energetic personalities, open-mindedness, and bravery. They have something unique to offer the world: they fearlessly express their inner truths through their curious minds and enthusiasm. Plus, they make great friends since they're funny and fun to be around. So, if you know a Sagittarius (or are one!), prepare for plenty of adventure, new experiences, and interesting conversations.

A. Glyph and Symbol

The glyph of Sagittarius is an Archer with its bow and arrow pointing up, symbolizing the sign's aim for success and its eagerness to explore new territory. Its symbol is the same.

B. Keywords

Energetic, Open-Minded, Brave

C. Element

Sagittarius is a Fire sign which symbolizes their natural passion and enthusiasm. It is associated with action, drive, and creative expression.

D. Modality

Sagittarius is a Mutable sign which means that the sign is focused on change, growth, and transformation. They adapt to their environment and always seek ways to expand their understanding of the world.

E. Planet

The ruling planet of Sagittarius is Jupiter, and its influence can be seen in the sign's optimism, faith, and expansive nature.

F. Polarity

Sagittarius is a Positive sign, meaning that they focus more on external sources of power than internal ones.

G. Correspondences

- Color: Light Blue
- Metal: Tin
- Stone: Turquoise
- Body Part: Hips.

Capricorn (December 22–January 19)

For all the Capricorns out there, you possess one of the most balanced and powerful signs of the zodiac. You can stay focused and organized in any situation. Your consistent behavior means you can carve a unique path to success through dedication, intelligence, and perseverance. As a hardworking Earth sign, you also appreciate creature comforts, making you an excellent provider for yourself and those close to you. Whether it's staying ahead of your personal goals or building relationships with others, Capricorn will surely bring out the best in any situation.

A. Glyph and Symbol

The glyph of Capricorn is a sea goat, representing the sign's ability to stay afloat in any situation and its ability to adapt. Its symbol is the same.

B. Keywords

Consistent, Dedicated, Intelligent, and Perseverance.

C. Element

Capricorn is an Earth sign which symbolizes their practicality and groundedness. It is associated with material comfort, stability, and reliability.

D. Modality

Capricorn is a Cardinal sign, which means that the sign is focused on initiating projects, leading others, and taking action. They are great at setting goals, taking advantage of opportunities, and getting things done.

E. Planet

The ruling planet of Capricorn is Saturn, and its influence can be seen in the sign's discipline, focus, and ambition.

F. Polarity

Capricorn is a Negative sign, meaning they are more focused on internal sources of power than external ones.

G. Correspondences

- Color: Brown
- Metal: Lead
- Stone: Onyx
- Body Part: The Knees.

Aquarius (January 20–February 18)

The Aquarius zodiac sign is a unique and interesting one in many ways. Represented by a water bearer, these individuals often possess visionary qualities that could be seen as ahead of their time. They bring a refreshing perspective to the world and tend to think differently than others in various situations. Those born under this sign typically have strong values and come off as quite independent, which gives them a strong aura of resilience. Because of their eccentric nature, Aquarius individuals are fearless problem-solvers known for being outstandingly creative. They are often intuitive and enjoy diving deep into the depths of complex conversations or thoughts. All in all, it's fair to say that having an Aquarius friend or member of your family can make life much more interesting.

A. Glyph and Symbol

Aquarius's glyph represents water, symbolizing the sign's ability to think deeply and unconventionally. Its symbol is the water bearer, which represents its willingness to offer something unique and valuable.

B. Keywords

Visionary, Independent, Resourceful, Creative.

C. Element

Aquarius is an Air sign which symbolizes the sign's inspiration, intellectualism, and originality. It is associated with communication, imagination, and freedom.

D. Modality

Aquarius is a fixed sign that focuses on maintaining and sustaining projects instead of just initiating them. They are great at staying consistent with their plans and following through with their goals.

E. Planet

The ruling planet of Aquarius is Uranus. Its influence can be seen in the sign's passion for progress and innovation.

F. Polarity

Aquarius is a Positive sign, meaning they are more focused on external sources of power than internal ones.

G. Correspondences

- Color: Electric Blue
- Metal: Uranium
- Stone: Amethyst
- Body Part: The Ankles.

Pisces (February 19–March 20)

Pisces is one of the most mysterious and compassionate zodiac signs. People born under this sign are always interested in helping, understanding, and supporting others in need. They have a profound ability to see the beauty in everyone else while also connecting with and understanding their own emotions. They are attentive listeners and great problem-solvers who always think outside the box to solve issues. What makes them unique is their ability to empathize deeply with someone and help them without judging or overwhelming them. Pisces will use its creativity and intuition to bring positivity into your life and help you overcome difficult times. Ultimately, Pisces is an old soul living in a modern world, a true beacon of hope for those around them.

A. Glyph and Symbol

The glyph of Pisces is a representation of two fishes, symbolizing the duality between emotions and reality. Its symbol is two fish tied together, representing the sign's ability to be in tune with themselves and others.

B. Keywords

Compassionate, Understanding, Empathetic, and Creative.

C. Element

Pisces is a Water sign which symbolizes the sign's deep emotions and intuition. It is associated with understanding, spiritualism, and sensitivity.

D. Modality

Pisces is a Mutable sign which means that the sign is well-suited for adapting to change and being flexible in different situations. They are great at trying new things and taking risks when needed.

E. Planet

The ruling planet of Pisces is Neptune, and its influence can be seen in the sign's dreamy outlook on life.

F. Polarity

Pisces is a Negative sign, meaning they are more focused on internal sources of power than external ones.

G. Correspondences

- Color: Sea-Green
- Metal: Platinum
- Stone: Aquamarine
- Body Part: The Feet

Just like each individual, every zodiac sign has aspects that make it unique and special. What's amazing about astrology is the way all the signs are connected. Something true for one sign might also hold true for another, even though the behavior of each sign can vary greatly. It's almost like astrology provides a secret language with which you can better understand yourself and those around you. Knowing how different zodiac signs interact with one another not only helps you to appreciate people better, but it encourages compassion and understanding as well. Whether you believe in astrology or not, it offers an interesting lens through which to view human nature and relationships.

The wheel of zodiac signs is a great way to learn about the twelve-sign zodiac system. It reminds us of how deeply we're connected and how energy travels through the various signs. We can see each sign's unique contribution, such as Aries being a blazing fire sign, Libra balancing the scales with justice, Scorpio digging deep into secrets, and Pisces providing a soothing water element. Not only does it help you to better understand yourself, your strengths, and your weaknesses, but it also helps you comprehend those around you. By looking at the powerful connections between the zodiacs, you can gain valuable insight into your relationships and create more harmonious connections in life.

Take the time to learn more about each sign so you can gain a better understanding of astrology and how it affects you. Studying the zodiac signs is an interesting and enlightening exercise that will help you determine how to best use your energies in life!

Chapter 5: Sun, Moon, and Rising Signs

Your zodiac sign represents certain traits and characteristics based on when you were born. This additional layer can bring even more insight into your personality. The sun sign details the basics of who you are, such as how you interact with the world around you. On the other hand, moon signs exemplify how your personality and values are formed by past events and experiences. Meanwhile, rising signs indicate your potential hidden talents and qualities, representing an innate functional state which is not influenced by your past. Knowing these can help you better understand yourself so you can live life more fully.

Each zodiac sign manifests differently as sun, moon, rising and descendant sign.
https://pixabay.com/es/photos/reloj-astronomico-praga-226897/

This chapter will discuss the role of each sign, as well as insights gained from each. It will also go through each of the 12 zodiac signs and explain how they manifest as sun, moon, rising, and descendant signs. From this, you should better understand your true self and the immense potential that lies within you. It is your job to unlock and use that potential to the fullest. While this can be difficult, the journey is well worth it.

Sun Signs

Have you ever wondered what astrological sign matches your personality? Sun signs are an interesting way to learn more about yourself and the people around you. They reveal a great deal about your character traits, from your best qualities to that one annoying habit you can't seem to shake. Knowing your sun sign also gives you an appreciation for how much we have in common with those born under the same sign, which is great food for thought. Whether you believe in it or not, exploring your sun sign can be quite beneficial! It's worth learning more and seeing how accurate they can be.

Role in Astrology

Sun Signs are an essential part of astrology, providing insight into the unique nature of each sign. People often ask how the position of the stars or planets affects their lives and personalities, and the answer is that it is all determined by astrological signs. They determine a person's zodiac sign, which reveals their tendencies, strengths, and weaknesses. Sun signs are mainly concerned with one's character traits and inner self instead of external events like job opportunities or relationships. Ultimately, looking at someone's sun sign can be a great way to learn more about who they are.

Insights Provided

One of the most enlightening insights that studying sun signs can provide is understanding your behavior, tendencies, and fate. Knowledge of the twelve zodiac signs allows you to gain a perspective on yourself and others. You can hear countless stories about others, learn how they approach life, and relate to their loved ones to broaden your understanding even more. Sun sign astrology deepens your connection with others by providing invaluable life insights. It can also help you make predictions by bringing structure and direction to where you are headed by symbolically interpreting timing using celestial movements.

Learning about individual characteristics associated with each of the astrological signs will provide further clarity about what patterns may arise next for you in your journey.

Moon Signs

Understanding what your moon sign is can give you greater insight into yourself, as it suggests how you react to your emotions and provides cues to how you deal with stress. It gives information about your inner life, clues about how well you manage personal relationships, giving an idea of who you are underneath the surface. In short, learning your moon sign helps you better grasp yourself and the relationships around you. With some investigation, knowledge, and practice, one can use the moon sign to develop a confident sense of self.

Role in Astrology

When it comes to astrology, moon signs can be incredibly enlightening. Moon signs can provide insight into your emotional makeup, helping you better understand how emotions influence your reactions and decisions. Whether you are familiar with the basics of astrology or have just discovered it for the first time, recognizing what your moon sign says about you will lead to more self-awareness and greater fulfillment. Each zodiac sign has its unique traits when it comes to emotions. With a deeper understanding of these traits, one can unlock new levels of self-knowledge that are truly powerful and transformative.

Insights Provided

It's easy to get caught up in the hustle and bustle of daily life, so taking a few moments to learn about your moon sign can give you clarity on how to approach each day. Knowing your moon sign enables you to better understand yourself and the motivations that drive you. It also builds stronger relationships with those around you by helping you recognize what drives their behavior. In addition, understanding your moon sign brings insight into the types of decisions that may bring positive outcomes or ones that will be difficult to recover from. All this knowledge can add up to a more meaningful and purposeful life if taken seriously and correctly used.

People often focus on sun signs, the day and month of your birth, but there's so much more than astrology has to offer. When you look into the placement of your moon sign in astrological houses, you can see what influences you emotionally and spiritually. Knowing this will help you find balance and inner peace in your life. The insight that moon signs can bring about one's emotions, habits, behaviors, and tendencies is invaluable, enabling us to learn our true purpose in life more deeply.

Rising Signs

Learning about your Rising Sign can be an eye-opening experience. Your Rising Sign is the sign of the zodiac associated with the degree of the eastern horizon at the time of your birth. Based on your location and time zone, it takes into account the precise position of the sun on Earth. Looking up your Rising Sign can give you an incredibly unique insight into what kind of person you are and why you have certain personality traits or perspectives that set you apart from others. Knowing more about your Rising Sign is a great way to understand yourself better and be proud of who you are!

Role in Astrology

In astrology, the rising sign has a crucial role to play. Often referred to as your "ascendant," it is the sign that was rising on the horizon at the exact moment of your birth and can tell you a lot about your external personality traits and how you present yourself to others. Rising signs explain why two people with similar sun signs may have drastically different personalities. Someone's rising sign truly makes them unique! The fact that all of this is determined by just one moment in time speaks to the incredible complexity and beauty of astrology.

Insights Provided

The rising sign, also known as the ascendant, provides a deeper level of self-knowledge and understanding. It is as crucial to an individual's birth chart as the Sun, Moon, and other planets. Your rising sign directly impacts how you relate to the world around you, your outlook on life, and your relationship with others. Knowing more about it can help provide insights into why certain complications or issues arise in areas such as relationships and career paths. With the right interpretation, it can reveal things like why we respond emotionally in a certain way or even why we feel something is lacking in a relationship. Seeking professional advice or taking some time to explore a birth chart can enable us to use our rising signs to gain greater clarity on ourselves and life's journey.

Descendants

Astrology is an ancient tradition with numerous applications and interpretations which can help you to better understand the world. One such area of study, particularly interesting in modern times, is the study of the Descendant in astrology. The descendant shows how you relate to and interact with those around you, including family, friends, and peers. It often reveals your hidden personality traits as well as how you show up in relationships of all kinds. Knowing these components of who you are can be extremely helpful for a person's journey in this life. Understanding the descendant and what it symbolizes can be tricky, but with a bit of research and exploration of astrology tools like charts or zodiac symbols, you, too, can learn more about yourself.

Role In Astrology

Many people have heard of a birth chart in astrology and know that it is divided into 12 sections, each representing an area of life. However, few know what the "Descendant" represents. The Descendant is the sign on the 7th house cusp and often symbolizes your relationships with others, both platonic and romantic. It can show unique aspects of your character, which may be found through intimate relationships or partnerships, along with how you go about creating those connections. People who are knowledgeable in astrology believe the Descendant plays a significant role in understanding yourself and even predicting your future.

Insights Provided

Astrology has many fascinating topics that can offer amazing insights into ourselves and our futures. One of these is the concept of a descendant, which traditionally marks the seventh house in an astrological chart. The descendant represents relationships in your life and how you operate within them and are perceived by others. It offers very valuable insights into yourself, such as how you handle intimacy, collaborations, and your one-on-one connections.

Additionally, it influences how we deal with public perceptions of us and allows us to be aware of potential issues. Knowing about your descendant within astrology can offer a lot of insight into your relationships and why you attract specific people or situations in your life. Understanding yourself better can lead to stronger and more fulfilling connections with those around you. So, get out there and learn about yours!

Zodiac Signs Revisited

It's time to revisit your beloved zodiac sign and explore what else can tell you about yourself! The traditional sun sign, determined by the month and date of your birthday, only gives a basic overview of someone's personality. A whole new layer of complexity is revealed when you look at people's birth charts based on the moon sign and rising sign. The moon sign symbolizes your innermost feelings and emotions, while the rising sign reveals how others experience you, and this combination creates a unique portrait of each individual. With an ever-changing universe around you impacting your daily life, taking into account your three signs together can help shed some light on what makes you tick.

Aries

Aries is a bold, passionate, and energetic sign that can bring an extra spark to any conversation, project, or situation.

As a Sun Sign

With Aries as your sun sign, you are full of courage and ambition, making you determined to get things done.

As a Moon Sign

Your moon sign reflects your emotions and the inner person you are. Aries moons are not afraid to express their moods, feel at ease, and be honest about life's ups and downs.

As a Rising Sign

Your rising sign is the public face you present to the world, which for Aries, might be represented by strength and determination. There's no stopping an Aries once they set their sights on something!

As A Descendant

Your Descendant reveals how you handle relationships as an Aries, and with this sign can come boldness when it comes to romantic pursuits. They tend to be fiercely loyal and passionate when it comes to their relationships. This can sometimes come off as intense, but they are ultimately looking to settle down with someone they truly love and trust.

Taurus

Taurus is a steady, reliable sign that often prefers to take it slow and steady.

As A Sun Sign

People with Taurus as their sun sign are often down-to-earth and have a strong sense of self-worth. They know what they need and aren't afraid to take what's theirs.

As a Moon Sign

Taurus moons feel strongly about their beliefs, rarely taking them lightly and often challenging those around them.

As a Rising Sign

A Taurian rising sign usually tells the world that this person is reliable and loyal, something that tends to attract admirers.

As a Descendant

Someone with Taurus as their descendant shows the world their need to be respected and appreciated. They are often looking for the same kind of steady love and support in their relationships as they give, rarely settling for anything less.

Gemini

Gemini is a dualistic sign that loves to explore the world around them.

As a Sun Sign

Geminis are inquisitive by nature, often having a passion for knowledge and the pursuit of adventure.

As a Moon Sign

Gemini moons are often quite sensitive and can be hard on themselves, making it difficult to open up to others.

As a Rising Sign

A Gemini rising sign usually indicates adaptability to new situations and people, making it easy for them to fit in quickly.

As a Descendant

Geminis with a descendant sign are often looking for someone to help bring their ideas and dreams to life. They can be fiercely passionate in their relationships and are always looking for something to explore and new heights to reach.

Cancer

Cancer is a nurturing sign that loves to take care of their loved ones.

As a Sun Sign

People with Cancer as their sun sign are often quite compassionate and caring, putting the needs of others first.

As a Moon Sign

Cancer moons are deeply emotional and can often be overwhelmed by their feelings.

As a Rising Sign

A Cancerian rising sign shows others that this person is kind and gentle, often looking out for the needs of those around them.

As a Descendant

Cancerians with a descendant sign typically show the world how much they need to feel deeply connected and loved in their relationships. They are often looking for someone who can share an emotional bond with them, someone who can understand their feelings and appreciate them for who they are.

Leo

Leo is an energetic sign that loves to be the center of attention.

As a Sun Sign

People with Leo as their sun sign are often confident and have a flare for being the center of attention.

As a Moon Sign

Leo moons can be quite expressive and often need to express themselves artistically.

As a Rising Sign

A Leonian rising sign might show others that this person is passionate and ambitious, often looking to make an impact on the world around them.

As a Descendant

Leos with a descendant sign are often looking for someone who can appreciate their boldness and enthusiasm. They need to be with someone who encourages them to keep striving forward while also providing them with the support and security they need to feel comfortable.

Virgo

Virgo is a practical sign that loves to help others.

As a Sun Sign

People with Virgo as their sun sign are often quite detail-oriented and strive for perfection.

As a Moon Sign

Virgo moons are analytical by nature and can often be hard on themselves, looking for ways to improve and grow.

As a Rising Sign

A Virgo rising sign usually shows that this person is organized and dependable, often taking on the role of helping others.

As a Descendant

Virgos with a descendant sign are often looking for someone who can help them find balance and stability in their relationships. They need to be with someone who is there for them when they need it while also giving them the freedom to grow and explore.

Libra

Libra is a harmonious sign that loves beauty and justice.

As a Sun Sign

People with Libra as their sun sign are often quite diplomatic and strive to keep the peace.

As a Moon Sign

Libra moons are often quite idealistic, looking for ways to bring balance and harmony into the world.

As a Rising Sign

A Libra rising sign usually indicates that this person is sociable and graceful, often looking to bring people together.

As a Descendant

Librans with a descendant sign typically need someone who can appreciate their big-picture thinking and help them stay grounded. They need to be with someone who is there for them when they need it while also giving them the freedom to express themselves.

Scorpio

Scorpio is an intense sign that loves to explore the depths of the unknown.

As a Sun Sign

People with Scorpio as their sun sign are often quite passionate and have a strong drive for transformation.

As a Moon Sign

Scorpio moons can be quite secretive and often need to explore their emotions to better understand themselves.

As a Rising Sign

A Scorpio rising sign usually indicates that this person is a mystery to outsiders, often looking to uncover the secrets of the world.

As a Descendant

Scorpios with a descendant sign are often looking for someone who can bring out their softer side while also understanding and respecting their need for privacy. They need to be with someone who can appreciate their intensity and passion while also giving them the space to explore their own emotions.

Sagittarius

Sagittarius is a philosophical sign that loves to explore the world.

As A Sun Sign

People with Sagittarius as their sun sign are often quite adventurous and seek out new experiences.

As A Moon Sign

Sagittarius moons are often quite optimistic and strive to bring joy and optimism into the world.

As a Rising Sign

A Sagittarian rising sign usually shows that this person is fun-loving and enthusiastic, often looking to expand their horizons.

As a Descendant

Sagittarians with a descendant sign often need someone who can encourage them to stay focused and grounded while also appreciating their love of learning and exploration. They need to be with someone who can bring balance and stability into their lives while also giving them the freedom to explore new ideas.

Capricorn

Capricorn is an ambitious sign that loves to take on new challenges.

As a Sun Sign

People with Capricorn as their sun sign are often quite goal-oriented and strive to achieve success.

As a Moon Sign

Capricorn moons can be quite serious and often need to find ways to connect with others to better understand themselves.

As a Rising Sign

A Capricornian rising sign usually indicates that this person is determined and practical, often looking to build something tangible.

As a Descendant

Capricorns with a descendant sign are often looking for someone who can bring out their softer side and help them relax and unwind. They need to be with someone who can provide guidance and support while also giving them the freedom to pursue their goals.

Aquarius

Aquarius is a curious sign that loves to explore the unknown.

As a Sun Sign

People with Aquarius as their sun sign are often quite progressive and strive to bring about positive change.

As a Moon Sign

Aquarius moons can be quite rebellious and often need to express their individuality to better understand themselves.

As a Rising Sign

An Aquarian rising sign usually indicates that this person is independent and progressive, often looking to push the boundaries of convention.

As a Descendant

Aquarians with a descendant sign are often looking for someone who can bring out their softer side and help them feel secure. They need to be with someone who can appreciate their uniqueness and individuality while also giving them the space to explore their ideas.

Pisces

Pisces is a compassionate sign that loves to help others.

As a Sun Sign

People with Pisces as their sun sign are often quite dreamy and strive to bring peace and balance into the world.

As a Moon Sign

Pisces moons can be quite sensitive and often need to express their emotions to better understand themselves.

As a Rising Sign

A Pisces rising sign usually indicates that this person is gentle and kind-hearted, often looking to nurture the people around them.

As a Descendant

Pisces with a descendant sign are often looking for someone who can bring out their strength and confidence. They need to be with someone who can encourage them to take risks and be assertive while also giving them the space to explore their own emotions.

Overall, each zodiac sign can manifest in different ways depending on its placement in the birth chart, so it's crucial to consider all of these factors when interpreting a person's astrological chart. By gaining a deeper understanding of the sun, moon, rising sign, and descendant in an individual's birth chart, you can gain insight into the person's character, qualities, and behaviors. Whether you are looking for guidance in your own life or want to better understand the people around you, delving into the world of astrology can be a great way to gain insight and clarity.

The knowledge in this chapter can provide a greater depth of understanding about how they communicate with others, their values and beliefs, their emotional needs and wants, as well as how they manifest their highest potential. With this knowledge increasing our awareness of these cosmic influences on each individual uniquely, we can develop more meaningful connections with those around us by appreciating the various intricacies that make up the people in our lives.

Chapter 6: The Houses I. Ego, Resources, and the Mind

Astrology is a fascinating study of the effects that planets, stars, and other celestial bodies have on physical and psychological life. One of its key components, which is sometimes overlooked, is the birth chart houses. Each house has an individual, symbolic meaning that speaks to different aspects of life, such as home, family, and relationships. These houses serve as a guideline for understanding and interpreting astrological information in a more personalized way. These insights can be conveniently combined with other astrological interpretations to get a full scope of how stars influence your life on Earth.

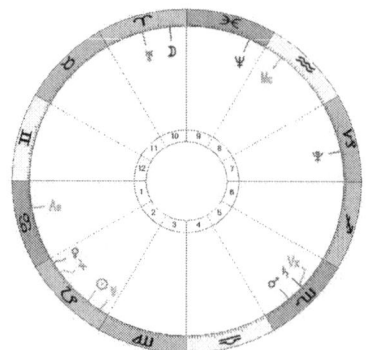

Astrological houses.
This file is licensed under the Creative Commons Attribution-Share Alike 4.0 International license. <https://creativecommons.org/licenses/by-sa/4.0/deed.en>
https://upload.wikimedia.org/wikipedia/commons/c/c7/Whole_Sign_house_divisions.jpg

This chapter will explore the individual houses of the birth chart. We will explore each house thoroughly by looking at cusps, keywords, themes, and the effects of different planets and zodiac signs in each house. Understanding each house gives you a better insight into how the stars influence your life on Earth. With this knowledge, each person can better understand their natural inclinations and motivators, using the planets' placement at their birth time.

Houses in Astrology

Astrology is a fascinating subject, full of depth and complexity. Did you know that it uses the concept of twelve houses to represent different aspects of life? These houses are used when interpreting an astrological chart, and each one speaks to a particular area, such as home, money, friends, career, and more. It's incredibly interesting how all of these specific areas of life can be characterized by an ancient symbolic system. Even if you're not an astrology enthusiast yourself, it's worth taking the time to appreciate how detailed and insightful this practice can be.

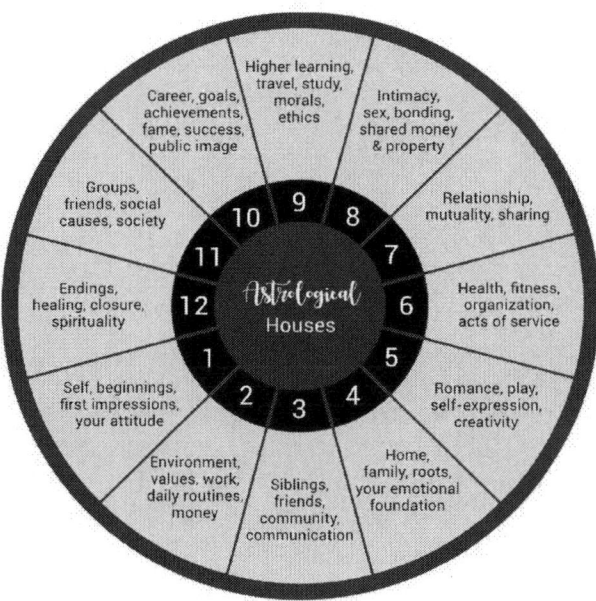

The 12 houses.

House Cusps

Have you ever noticed similarities between people with the same astrology sign? It turns out there is more to interpreting your birth chart than just knowing your sun sign! The concept of house cusps in astrology adds another layer to create a more comprehensive picture of who you are and how the universe shapes you. House cusps are the points that divide your natal chart into 12 sections (or houses); each represents certain aspects of your personality. By studying where powerful planets like Jupiter and Saturn fall about the house cusps, you can gain valuable insights into how your energy plays off against different parts of life, helping you to understand more about yourself and others.

Theme

The theme of the houses is dependent on the house in question. The first house, for example, is known as the "house of ego" and speaks to themes like self-expression, identity, and early life experiences. The second house is known as the "house of resources" and speaks to themes like money, possessions, and material security. The third house, meanwhile, is known as the "house of mind" and speaks to themes like communication, education, and siblings. In general, each house speaks to a particular part of life, with the zodiac sign ruling that house plays a major role in how it is interpreted.

Planet/Sign Analysis

The zodiac sign ruling each house plays a major role in how it is interpreted. For example, if your birth chart has Aries ruling the first house, you can expect to have a strong sense of courage and independence in your life. If Scorpio rules the eighth house, then you can expect to have keen insights into the depths of yourself and others. In addition, the planets in each house also play a role in how it is interpreted. Planets like the Sun, which represents our ego identity, can give you an insight into how you express and interact with others in the world. Meanwhile, the Moon, which represents your inner emotions and subconscious desires, can give you an insight into how you relate to yourself on a deeper level.

The First House: Ego

The first house in astrology symbolizes the ego or how a person presents themselves to the world. This is an important factor in determining a person's fate and destiny throughout life. It's no surprise that those with strong first houses tend to project their confidence and inner will powerfully to make an impact on the world around them. For those with weak first houses, it can pay to put in some extra effort to get yourself out without feeling judged or labeled by others. After all, humans are here for a short time, so make sure you express yourself.

Ruling Zodiac Sign and Planet

Aries, the first sign of the zodiac, and Mars, the planet of ambition and drive, both gracefully rule the first house. With the combination of the two great forces, this house contains a warrior-like energy that is unparalleled. People guided by this power are formidable forces to be reckoned with who dare to take on life's difficult challenges without retreating or wrapping up in their comfort zone. Those born under Aries and Mars know that no challenge is too great for them to tackle as long as they use their inner strength and determination to reach their goals. There may be times along the way when big obstacles arise, but that fiery energy will not falter until success is obtained.

House Cusps and Meaning

The house cusp of the first house is known as the Ascendant (also called the Rising sign). It marks the beginning of your journey into the world and provides a clue as to how You'll approach life. The Descendant, meanwhile, marks the end of your journey in the world and gives you insight into how you will leave your mark.

Medium Coeli (MC) and Imum Coeli (IC) are two other important points in the chart which are related to the house cusps. MC represents your public persona, while IC speaks to your private persona. These points can give you insight into how the outside world views you and the inner parts of yourself that remain hidden.

Main Keywords

The main keywords associated with the first house are ambition, purpose, identity, self-expression, and courage.

Description of the House's Theme

The first house represents a person's character, personality, and approach to life. It speaks to how you express yourself, your motivations and goals, and how you interact with others. This is the house of ego where you form your identity and project it out into the world. It is also a house of courage and inner will, as it takes guts to stand up for yourself and take risks to make an impact. The first house speaks to the very foundations of your being, and it is important to pay attention to how you present yourself to the world.

Planet/Sign Analysis

The ruling planet and the sign of the first house play a major role in how it is interpreted. The sign of Aries and planet Mars gives the first house its fiery energy, emphasizing ambition, strength, and a desire to take risks to make an impact. The Sun, meanwhile, is the planet of identity and ego, and it gives you insight into how you express yourself to the world. The Moon also plays an important role as it represents your inner emotions and subconscious desires. It helps you understand your relationship with yourself and how you can nurture it to grow and become the best version of yourself.

Overall, the first house is a powerful tool to explore your identity and how it affects your life journey. It provides insight into how you present yourself to the world and how you can use your inner fire and courage to make an impact. Paying attention to this house can help you to understand yourself better and take control of your destiny.

The Second House: Resources

The second house of astrology is known as the house of resources, and it deals with money, possessions, self-confidence, and material security. It clarifies how you utilize your resources for growth and stability. This house affects profit through work, inheritance, taxes, investments, the increased value of assets, and pay raises. Your concern for tangible valuables such as physical objects, wealth, acquisitions, and comfort items also falls under this section. This house also reflects your capacity to hold on to or let go of the material things in your life with acceptance or resolutions. Astrology can help you to understand how your financial decisions may be influenced by the planets and lead you to form a successful approach to managing resources both materially and psychologically.

Ruling Zodiac Sign and Planet

The Second House is one of the most interesting places to explore in the celestial sky. This house is ruled by the Zodiac sign of Taurus, along with the planet Venus. It helps you look into how you use money and other resources to ensure your security and where your values come from. Plus, it can provide insights into what type of possessions bring you joy, material or otherwise. Knowing your second house can organize your finances and make sure that you're making wise decisions when it comes to spending and saving; exploring it will expand your cosmic consciousness.

House Cusps and Meaning

The cusp of the second house is known as the "Cadent," and it speaks to your ability to manage resources, both materially and psychologically. It is associated with the concept of "wealth," and it reflects your capacity to hold on to or let go of material things in your life.

Main Keywords

The main keywords associated with the second house are resources, money, possessions, self-confidence, and material security.

Description of the House's Theme

The second house is all about material security, how you use your resources to create wealth, and your capacity to manage money. It represents what you own in the physical world and how you use it to create stability for yourself. This house also speaks to your self-esteem and how you feel about your worth. It reflects the kind of relationship you have with money, possessions, and physical objects and how those relationships can either help or hinder them. By understanding the second house, you can gain insight into how you can use your resources to create the kind of life you want for yourself.

Planet/Sign Analysis

Taurus and Venus are the rulers of the second house, and their influence can be seen in how we handle our resources. Taurus is a sign of stability and practicality, encouraging you to take a practical approach to money and possessions. Venus is the planet of values, and it helps you to understand what you value in life and how you can use your resources to create stability. When these two planets are combined, they give you the ability to manage your resources practically and meaningfully.

Overall, the second house of astrology can be a powerful tool for understanding your relationship with money and possessions. It provides insight into how you can use your resources to create the kind of life you desire and build the stability you need for long-term success. By paying attention to this house, you can better understand your finances and how you can use them to create the kind of life you want.

The Third House: The Mind

The third house of astrology is a fascinating realm of study. Ruling the realm of information and the mind can be seen as a gateway to understanding how you interact with the world around you. It looks at the things that affect your decisions and actions, from communication to education to which theories you hold true. As humans, you must examine every part of your life to evolve and grow. Examining the third house is one way to do just that. With deeper knowledge comes a greater connection to yourself, and unlocking the secrets of this mysterious place can lead you to major discoveries about yourself and your world.

Ruling Zodiac Sign and Planet

The third house, also known as the house of the mind, is ruled by the zodiac sign Gemini and the planet Mercury. Ruled by Gemini, this house is related to communication, mental connections between people, thoughts, ideas, and beliefs you hold to be true. Think about it, Gemini is always on the go, socializing and chatting as it loves exchanging ideas! Meanwhile, Mercury calls for clear thinking. It pertains to your ability to process information quickly and apply intelligence reliably. Overall, this house deals with how you make sense of information mentally and verbally.

House Cusps and Meaning

The cusp of the third house, known as the "Succedent," is all about information, how you take it in, and how you process it. It represents the way you learn, think, and express your thoughts.

Main Keywords

The main keywords associated with the third house are communication, education, networking, learning, and analysis.

Description of the House's Theme

The third house is the realm of communication, intellectual pursuits, and learning. Here, you can explore your thought processes, how you take in information, and how you express yourself to the world. It is a house of education, understanding how you use your knowledge to make sense of the world around you and how you interact with others. It looks at how you learn and use your knowledge to grow. It also speaks to your ability to connect with others, understand their perspectives, and build meaningful relationships.

Planet/Sign Analysis

Gemini and Mercury are the rulers of the third house, and their influence can be seen in how we think and communicate. Gemini is a sign of intelligence and communication, encouraging you to explore new ideas and express yourself without fear. Mercury is the planet of logic and reason, helping you make sense of the world around you and understand different perspectives. When these two planets are combined, they give you the tools to think critically and communicate ideas effectively.

Overall, the third house of astrology is a powerful tool for understanding how you think, communicate, and learn. It provides insight into your intellectual pursuits and the way you take in information from the world around you. By examining this house, you can better understand your thought process and how it shapes your actions.

Exploring the houses of astrology can be an illuminating experience, providing insight into all areas of life, from behavior patterns to relationships. Looking deeper into each one can give you a better understanding of your personality and the motivation for different choices and experiences. They even advise how you can respond to the challenges and opportunities that come your way.

Looking at the houses of astrology can provide you with invaluable wisdom that might otherwise remain unknown, often giving more satisfying answers than "just follow your gut." With this knowledge, we can gain greater insight into ourselves and how we interact with the world. By exploring the houses of astrology, you can better understand how you move through life and the choices that come your way.

Chapter 7: The Houses II. Home, Creativity, and Health

Astrology has been around for centuries and fascinates and influences people even today. The concept of houses, composed of 12 divisions, indicates where a celestial body (like the sun or the moon) is positioned relative to your life at a given moment in time. The various astrological houses each represent different areas of your life. Knowing and understanding this information can be incredibly valuable to gain deeper insight into yourself, as it provides an objective look into your past, present, and future circumstances.

This chapter will focus on the fourth, fifth, and sixth astrological houses. It will dive into each of these houses to explore them thoroughly. It will also look at the ruling zodiac sign and planet, house cusps and their meanings, the main keywords that describe them, a description of each house's theme, and a brief analysis of the effects and lessons of each planet and zodiac sign in that house. With this knowledge, you can work through any difficulties or issues that life throws at you more effectively.

The Fourth House: The Home

The fourth astrological house is often thought of as where the soul's most intimate home lies. Rich with symbolism and cultural significance, studying this house has the potential to offer powerful insights into the individual and the role their home plays in their life. Many look to this house to uncover what they prioritize and value, with various aspects within it, across boundaries, communication, siblings, and transportation, helping people work out not only how these things have impacted them personally but how they can use them going forward to achieve their goals.

From an astrological viewpoint, the concept of "home" spans far beyond the physical aspects of having a roof over your head and the security it affords you. Home is so much more than just tangible property. It's about how you attach yourself to space, people, and places and energetically connect in ways that shape how you exist on a grand scale. Moving from this perspective allows you to get a fuller understanding of home as part of your unique map on this Earth.

With some reflection and exploration, you can see how each area has its own set of archetypes, traditions, environmental conditions, and world view that greatly shapes your experience in life. Understanding these dynamics can add tremendous richness to the idea of home and provide even deeper insight into who you are as an individual.

Ruling Zodiac Sign and Planet

Gemini and its ruling planet, Mercury, are an interesting combination. When these two heavenly bodies work together, they can bring a wide variety of influences to the fourth house. Outgoing Gemini energy supplies the inquisitiveness for wanting to learn and explore, while Mercury provides the communication skills, clear thinking, and mental agility necessary for information gathering. As such, expect plenty of intellectual stimulation regarding all matters related to this house.

House Cusps and Their Meaning

The cusp of the fourth house is usually associated with the sign of Gemini, and it is often referred to as the "Gemini Gate." This cusp marks a pivotal point in life's journey, as it signifies the beginning of self-expression and exploration. The cusp of Gemini is a starting point for any new idea, concept, or belief system. It's the point at which you can start applying your knowledge and understanding of the world around you to find your place.

Main Keywords

The main keywords for the fourth astrological house are communication, ideas, information, exploration, travel, and siblings. The fourth astrological house is all about communicating, expanding your intellectual horizons, connecting with others, and exploring new places. It's a great opportunity to expand your knowledge and understanding of the world around us. The main keywords associated with this house are all potential growth areas for anyone who chooses to pay attention to them. Whether it means exchanging stories with a sibling or embarking on a journey far from home, this house encourages you to explore the world around you to make the most of your life.

Description of the House's Theme

The fourth house is all about communication and the exchange of ideas. It is also associated with travel and exploration, representing the desire to venture into the world and gain knowledge. The fourth house has a strong connection to siblings, as it is the house of early childhood and family development. This house is a place of growth and learning where individuals can expand their minds and discover new perspectives.

Planet/Sign Analysis

Mercury has a strong influence over the fourth house, as it is associated with communication and understanding. With its powers of eloquence, quick wit, and mental agility, Mercury can help an individual gain a greater understanding of the world around them. This is further enhanced when its influence is combined with that of Gemini, the sign associated with this house. Gemini energy is curious and eager to explore, making it a perfect match for Mercury's more intellectual and analytical side. These two forces can create a powerful combination that leads to greater personal growth and understanding.

The sign Gemini is also associated with siblings and this house, as it reflects the connection between two people. This relationship can be a source of great joy, but it can also be a source of conflict. Gemini energy encourages open dialogue and understanding, which can help to resolve any issues that arise. It is also a sign of exploration and learning, which can lead to discoveries and insights. Finally, Gemini can also be a great source of encouragement and support as it encourages individuals to reach their full potential.

Overall, the fourth house is about communication, exploration, and a better understanding of oneself and the world around them. It is a place of growth and learning where individuals can find new perspectives and gain greater insight into their own identities. Through its connection to the planet Mercury and the sign Gemini, this house can provide an abundance of mental stimulation and exploration that leads to personal growth.

The Fifth House: Creativity

The fifth house of Astrology is a fascinating area of study that explores the creative energies within us. This house focuses on creative areas like hobbies, artistic expression, and even hospitality. It's the part within you that allows you to be creative and try new things. It's also associated with your innermost emotions and feelings of home and family, which can greatly influence your creative endeavors. Exploring this house can lead to discovering hidden talents and a newfound appreciation for your innate creativity.

By recognizing the fifth house in astrology, you can answer questions like "what drives me? What abilities do I possess? How do I recreate my life and discover who I truly am?" This knowledge allows for a greater understanding of yourself and your relationships with others. So why not leap and dive into this mystical world of insight? You may be surprised at the power of your imagination when coupled with cosmic wisdom.

Ruling Zodiac Sign and Planet

The fifth house is ruled by the zodiac sign of Cancer and the planet Moon. The influence of these two planets gives this house an emotionally charged energy, as the Moon governs our innermost feelings and emotions. Cancer energy is also strongly associated with home, comfort, and security, providing a safe and nurturing environment for creativity to flourish. This combination of energies allows for a profound connection with the inner self and encourages individuals to explore their full potential.

House Cusps and Meaning

The fifth house is represented by the cusps of Imum Coeli and Medium Coeli. Imum Coeli, Latin for "the lowest of the heavens," represents the bottom tier of the zodiac and is associated with home, family, and inner feelings. This cusp is a gateway to the soul and encourages individuals to explore their spiritual side. On the other hand, Medium Coeli, Latin for "the middle of the heavens," is associated with intellectual pursuits and higher education. This cusp allows for exploration into the world of knowledge and encourages individuals to broaden their horizons.

Main Keywords

The main keywords for the fifth house are creativity, home, emotions, family, inner feelings, exploration, and spirituality. It's certainly a place of comfort and solace, but it is capable of so much more. Every part of this house holds something special, from the creativity it brings out in people to its ability to nurture family life and emotions. It helps one explore the depths of their inner feelings through its spiritual guidance, creating a space where one can feel secure and at home with themselves. With all these beautiful aspects, it's no wonder why many people who come into contact with the fifth house feel so connected.

Description of House Theme

The fifth house in astrology is about discovering the creative potential within us. It encourages individuals to explore their innermost emotions and life's possibilities. This house is also associated with home and family, which can serve as a strong source of guidance and support to those who seek it. This house's energies allow you to express your feelings and discover a newfound appreciation for yourself.

Planet/Sign Analysis

The energy of the Moon and Cancer gives the fifth house a strong emotional charge. The Moon, associated with feminine energy, is all about connecting to your innermost feelings and emotions. Conversely, cancer is associated with home and family life, which can give you a greater sense of security and stability. Together, these energies can help individuals to explore their creative potential in a safe and nurturing environment. With the Moon's influence, you can tap into your innermost desires and express yourself meaningfully. With the energy of Cancer, you can find comfort and security in your family life, allowing you to explore your creative talents with a greater sense of ease.

The fifth house in astrology encourages individuals to explore their inner world and tap into their true potential. By recognizing the importance of home and family, you can discover a newfound appreciation for your creative talents and better understand yourself and your relationships with others. With the energy of Cancer and the Moon, you can explore your innermost feelings in a safe and nurturing environment and tap into your creative potential. By exploring the fifth house in astrology, you can gain greater insight into yourself and be more in tune with your emotions. This can ultimately help you find your creative voice and unlock your potential.

The Sixth House: Health

The sixth house of astrology, the House of Health, indicates how healthy and strong we are in our bodies. This house is thought to be connected to our overall physical state as well as our vitality. It also plays a role in detailing where your health weaknesses may lie. To evaluate your health from an astrological point of view, you'll need to take a look at this house and observe how the different planets are placed within it. This will help you figure out what health challenges might be present in your life and offer advice on ways to stay healthy and alert. Keep in mind that staying physically active, eating right, and getting enough sleep can go a long way in helping you remain healthy overall.

Ruling Zodiac Sign and Planet

The sixth house, ruled by Leo and the Sun, is an area of your chart that inherently focuses on enjoyment. This can be anything from creative hobbies to deep-seated passions, allowing you to take a break from life's struggles and just have fun. Leo's influence suggests here it's all about celebrating the best bits of yourself, your confident persona, and the brave new ideas that help shape who you are. It's a place to feel truly alive, bask in your light, and show yourself some love. With the Sun as ruler of this part of your journey, make sure you take time out of every day to take pleasure in life.

Main Keywords

While it may not be the most-talked-about house, this house has some interesting things to offer. It's connected to health, vitality, energy, and physical well-being. So, if you're feeling out of sorts or need to hit the reset button on your own wellness goals, this could be a great spot to check out in your astrological chart. It also brings pleasure, joy, creativity, leisure activities (think yoga and painting classes), and general happiness. So, remember that if you're looking for some enthusiasm and satisfaction, the sixth house just might be the answer!

Description of the House's Theme

The sixth house in astrology is associated with overall health and well-being. It speaks to the vitality that you have within yourself, as well as your physical strength. This house can also reveal areas of weakness within your health and how to address these issues. Additionally, it speaks to the pleasure and joy you experience through creative hobbies, passions, and leisure activities. The sixth house is a place to celebrate the best parts of yourself, bask in your light, and be nurturing toward yourself. It's also a place to explore new ideas and activities that help shape your identity.

Planet/Sign Analysis

The Sun, the ruler of this house, is associated with creativity and joy. It allows you to explore your creative side and take pleasure in life. With the Sun in this house, you can feel energized and alive when expressing yourself through your passions and hobbies. Leo is also associated with this house, which brings a sense of confidence and boldness. It encourages you to be your true self and enjoy being unique. With this sign, you can feel fearless in your pursuits and find the courage to take risks. The Moon is associated with nurturing and caring for yourself, which is key to health and well-being. This planet helps you to take a closer look at your emotions, allowing you to tap into your needs and prioritize yourself.

Overall, the sixth house in astrology helps you gain insight into your physical health and overall sense of joy and pleasure. It encourages you to explore your passions, take risks, and be confident. By tapping into the energies of this house, you can learn to prioritize your health and well-being and find joy in life's little pleasures.

The fourth house in astrology is a powerful space that speaks about your home, family, and daily routines. By taking a closer look at this house, you can gain insight into how you interact with your environment and the people around you. You can also gain insight into your overall sense of joy and pleasure, allowing you to take time out of life's struggles and have fun.

The fifth house in astrology is an equally powerful space connected to your creativity, passions, and leisure activities. By tapping into this house's energies, you can learn to prioritize your health and well-being, take risks, and find joy in life's little pleasures. Ultimately, the sixth house reminds you to take time out of your day for your health and well-being, as well as for creative pursuits and leisure activities. By exploring this house, you can better understand yourself and how you are connected to the world around you.

Chapter 8: The Houses III. Relationships, Growth, and Travel

The astrological houses are an essential part of any astrological study. Through these twelve houses, you gain insight into yourself and your surroundings. Each house has its unique meaning, characterized by the planetary ruler it is associated with. Studying the houses can allow you to better understand both the cosmic energies at work within your life and how they affect people close to you. This knowledge can provide deeper insight into relationships, life paths, goals, and more. The astrological houses make it possible to understand yourself at a whole new level.

This chapter will dive into the zodiac's seventh, eighth, and ninth houses and explain their meanings in detail. It will start by exploring the seventh house, which is all about relationships. It will then move on to the eighth house, which focuses on growth and transformation. Finally, the ninth house, which is all about travel and higher learning, will be discussed. Each house will be analyzed regarding its ruling zodiac sign and planet, house cusps and their meanings, main keywords, a description of the house's theme, and finally, a brief analysis of each planet/sign in the house. By the end, you should better understand astrological houses and how they affect your life.

The Seventh House: Relationships

The seventh astrological house is all about relationships and covers every type of relationship you can think of. From deep romantic love to lifelong friendships to working partnerships with your colleagues, this house of the zodiac can tell you a lot about your connection with others. It looks at how you come together and combines your strengths and how you handle communication in relationships. You can learn a lot from analyzing the seventh house, allowing you to connect better with the people around you. So why not look up what it reveals about your relationships and discover how to strengthen them?

Ruling Zodiac Sign and Planet

The seventh house is ruled by Libra and also by Venus. Libra, the sign of balance, harmony, and justice, helps you to understand how to nurture relationships. Venus, the planet of love and beauty, encourages you to seek out relationships that bring peace and joy.

House Cusps and Their Meaning

The seventh house is cusped by the Descendant and the Medium Coeli (MC). The Descendant marks the beginning of the seventh house, indicating where you are open to new relationships. The Medium Coeli is the highest point in this house, symbolizing the pinnacle of success in a relationship. It also shows what you can learn from your relationships and how you can use them to grow.

Main Keywords

The seventh astrological house has so much to offer in terms of analyzing interpersonal relationships. The main keywords associated with the seventh astrological house are relationships, partnerships, commitments, compromise, communication, and balance. This house helps you unpack the challenges and celebrations that come with sharing life with another person, whether a love partner, family member – or even a pet.

Here you make commitments, both big and small, and can identify areas where compromise is necessary. To ensure smooth communication and balanced relationships, it is essential to understand how your needs relate to another's to achieve strong dynamic partnerships. The seventh house is where we can begin learning this valuable lesson. The seventh house teaches you that relationships are a two-way street and you should never be afraid to speak up for yourself.

Description of the House's Theme

The seventh astrological house is where relationships and partnerships take the spotlight. This house focuses on understanding your own needs, as well as those of your partner, on creating a balanced and healthy relationship. It is here that you learn how to compromise with others while also staying true to yourself. This house looks at the dynamics of a relationship, from its beginnings to its inevitable end. It also teaches you that all relationships will have their ups and downs and that it is important to communicate effectively to navigate any issues that come up.

Planet/Sign Analysis

Libra, the ruler of the seventh house, encourages us to aim for harmony and balance in our relationships. Libra helps you recognize what you need from a partner and what you can bring to the table. Venus, also ruling this house, is the planet of love and beauty. It inspires you to nurture your relationships and make them stronger. Both planets help you to understand how your relationships can benefit from communication, compromise, and mutual understanding. No matter what kind of relationship you are looking to nurture, the seventh house can help you find a way.

By diving deeper into the seventh house, you can gain insight into your relationships and learn how to make them stronger. From understanding the dynamics of a relationship to finding balance, the seventh house is full of knowledge that can help you grow. By exploring this house, you can become better connected with the people you care about and create lasting relationships.

The Eighth House: Growth

The eighth house in astrology has a mystique all its own. It is associated with transformation and growth, allowing you to go through powerful changes which allow for accelerated personal growth. Additionally, the eighth house rules health, finance, and sex, the latter of which will forever remain shrouded in mystery. It can be uncomfortable thinking about those topics in detail or even at all, but it can be eye-opening when you do so with an open mind. Examining your life through the lens of this mysterious house has tremendous potential to unlock hidden meanings and deepen your understanding of life.

It's related to the idea of transformation and speaks to the depth of your life as you enter into a space that touches upon taboo topics such as sexuality and death. This eighth house is all about getting down to the nitty-gritty details of life and experiencing evolution through challenging times. By facing mortality and embracing sex as a natural part of being human, you can embrace growth in a way that takes you to deeper levels of self-knowledge. Understanding this house opens up a path for you to understand yourself even more!

Ruling Zodiac Sign and Planet

The eighth house is ruled by Scorpio and Pluto, both of which carry a connotation of mystery and darkness. They can represent confronting and uncomfortable aspects of life that we may prefer to avoid. However, although this house can bring with it some difficult lessons and uncertainties, it also brings powerful growth opportunities. Pluto's transformative energy can be incredibly empowering if we let it. Scorpio encourages you to dig deep into the depths of your psyche and uncover the hidden parts of yourself that you may not even want to admit exist.

House Cusps and Their Meaning

The eighth house's cusp points are the midheaven and the ascendant. The midheaven, also referred to as Medium Coeli, is associated with our public lives and our aspirations. It speaks to what we hope to achieve in life but also carries the potential for transformation and growth. The ascendant, or Imum Coeli, is related to your personal lives and how you interact with the world around you. It reflects your personality, how you present yourself to the world, and how you take in information from your environment.

Main Keywords

The eighth house in astrology is associated with life's more complex and challenging traits. Transformation, growth, regeneration, and renewal are all keywords that reflect the constant cycle of change - but this house also covers taboos like mortality, death, and sex. Far from being an area to be overlooked, these themes provide a unique opportunity for a greater understanding of your life and how you interact with yourself and others. This can be a stimulating journey of mastery as you peel back the mysteries of the eighth house!

Description of the House's Theme

The eighth house in astrology is a powerful and mysterious force. This house is all about transformation, challenging your beliefs, and exploring the depths of your psyche. It covers difficult topics such as mortality, death, and sex in a way that allows you to confront these areas of your life with understanding and acceptance. Despite the difficult nature of these topics, embracing the eighth house can be incredibly rewarding as it provides you with a greater understanding of yourself and your place in the world.

Planet/Sign Analysis

The eighth house is ruled by Scorpio, which carries with it a sense of transformation and change. Although it may seem daunting, embracing the energy of Scorpio can allow you to explore your innermost desires and find a path to personal growth. The sign's strong connection with sex provides you with an opportunity to understand your sexuality better and what it means for you as an individual.

The ruling planet, Pluto, is all about power and control. It can be difficult to confront areas of your life that you may fear, but Pluto's energy gives you the strength to move forward. It also speaks to your ability to regenerate and find new life in the wake of death. By embracing Pluto's energy, you can find the strength and courage to confront and overcome your fears.

Ultimately, understanding the eighth house provides you with a greater insight into yourself and your journey in life. It allows you to confront difficult topics such as death and sexuality while at the same time providing you with growth opportunities. With its mysterious and powerful energy, the eighth house can be an incredibly rewarding area of astrology to explore.

The Ninth House: Travel

The ninth astrological house is associated with knowledge, expanding mental horizons, and pursuing spiritual truth. It also focuses on the development of a better understanding of yourself and how you interact with the world around you. So, if you feel the urge to set off on an adventure and explore new places, physically or emotionally, perhaps it's the ninth astrological house whispering through your head! And why not? Experiencing different cultures has a way of broadening your perspectives, helping you learn more about yourself and others all at once.

The ninth astrological house is an area of focus that can bring great depth and meaning to our lives. It speaks to your sense of wonder and adventure and offers space for reflection and understanding. Travel teaches you about different cultures, exposes you to different perspectives, and enhances your ability to communicate with those you encounter. Whether you are a globetrotter or a day tripper, this house brings forth opportunities for new experiences that you can take with you forever.

Ruling Zodiac Sign and Planet

The ninth house is ruled by Sagittarius and its ruling planet, Jupiter. Jupiter symbolizes luck, expansion, and opportunity, all qualities essential for successful exploration. With Jupiter's influence, you are more likely to find luck and abundance on your travels, allowing you to be more open to new experiences and possibilities.

Sagittarius is the sign of exploration and knowledge. This sign encourages you to go beyond your comfort zone and seek out information that is different from yours. By embracing the energy of Sagittarius, you can become more open to learning and exploring, allowing you to return from your travels with a broader understanding of the world.

House Cusps and Their Meaning

The ninth house cusp (Medium Coeli) is associated with the moon's south node and symbolizes your past. This point speaks to the experiences you have had in the past that shape your present and future. The Imum Coeli (the lowest point of the chart) marks the north node of the moon and speaks to your future. This point symbolizes potential and opportunity, showing you where you can go in life if you seize the chance. It encourages you to take risks, explore new possibilities, and make the most of your experiences.

Main Keywords

The ninth astrological house is often said to be associated with luck, journeys, discovery, and the search for knowledge. Whether that means looking inward for spiritual truths or venturing out onto foreign lands and cultures, this house has something in store for everyone. You may never know the fullness of life, but with ongoing self-discovery and a curiosity for what lies beyond you, you can be sure that every moment is captivating. Exploring this incredible space can help reinvigorate your thoughts, broaden your perspectives, and open you up to new possibilities that you may have never anticipated.

Description of the House's Theme

The ninth astrological house is a space for exploration and discovery. It encourages you to go beyond your comfort zones and seek out knowledge in all its forms. It speaks to your sense of wonder, curiosity, and ability to learn from the experiences you have had in life. With the ninth house, you can open yourself up to new perspectives, broaden your understanding and uncover the mysteries of life. The ninth house also speaks to your ability to make the most out of opportunities and take advantage of luck when it comes your way. Whether you find yourself on a new journey or simply exploring the depths of your mind, this house has something to offer you.

Planet/Sign Analysis

Jupiter in the ninth house offers us luck and abundance, encouraging us to go out and discover new things. When Jupiter is strong in your chart, you are more likely to experience success and opportunity on your travels. In the ninth house, Sagittarius encourages you to be open-minded and seek knowledge. This sign encourages you to question the status quo and learn from the experiences of others. When you embrace the energy of Sagittarius, you are more likely to open yourself up to new perspectives and expand your understanding of the world.

By exploring the ninth house, you can discover more about yourself and the world around you. You can open your mind to new possibilities and experience life in a way that you never thought possible. By diving into this space, you can find abundance and opportunity, allowing you to continue your journey of discovery for a lifetime.

The seventh, eighth, and ninth astrological houses offer us a tremendous chance to look further into our inner and outer worlds. These are the houses of relationships, growth, and travel, where you start to get in touch with yourself and how you connect with other people. From what it says about your deepest desires, revealing the way you grieve, or giving insight into your quest for success, understanding these three houses can give you a better understanding of yourself, your motivation, and how you navigate life. Even if you're unfamiliar with astrology, exploring these houses is an invaluable opportunity that can awaken amazing new things in you.

Each house is filled with its meaning, symbolism, and lessons, giving you a chance to uncover something new about yourself and your place in this world. By tapping into the energy of these three houses, you can open yourself up to a new realm of possibility and start to make sense of your life. With an open mind, a brave heart, and a willingness to explore, diving into the seven, eighth and ninth houses can be one of the most transformative experiences you can have in life.

Chapter 9: The Houses IV. Career, Friendship, and Spirituality

Astrological houses are an exciting way to learn about yourself and your journey through life. These areas of a natal chart teach you about your character, how you relate to others, and what the future has in store. They can provide powerful insight into the paths you may take, allowing you to gain clarity regarding your decisions and potential outcomes. Exploring these astrological houses can be an interesting experience that gives you a better understanding of who you are and why certain situations manifest in your life.

This chapter will explore the tenth, eleventh, and twelfth houses of a natal chart. It will dive into each house to look at the ruling zodiac sign and planet, house cusps and their meanings, main keywords that describe it, and a description of the house's theme that goes in-depth on what it signifies. It will also look at the effects and lessons of each planet and the zodiac sign in the house. If you're looking to deepen your understanding of career, friendship, and spirituality in your chart, this chapter is for you.

The Tenth House: Career

When it comes to making choices about your career, look no further than the tenth astrological house. This influential house gives us insight into our professional paths and provides hints as to which direction we should go. It's all about mapping out what you want to achieve while on this earth, no matter how big or small. The tenth house is filled with potential opportunities that could push you further than you ever thought possible. Take a few moments to read up on the tenth house and see what messages it has for you. Knowing yourself is key to finding success and happiness, so be sure to understand the knowledge it can bring before deciding which path you should take when investing in your career.

Ruling Zodiac Sign and Planet

The tenth astrological house is ruled by both Capricorn and Saturn. These two powerful forces give you the necessary perseverance and determination to reach your goals. They also teach you important lessons about self-discipline, structure, and focus. Capricorn is the zodiac sign of career, and Saturn brings in a sense of authority and responsibility. Together, they provide you with the tools to make wise decisions regarding your career choices. The combination of these two energies brings stability, ambition, and wisdom.

The properties of the tenth house govern work-related matters like career decisions or public reputation. An individual's goals for success are given an extra boost when Jupiter travels through this house, as chances for personal advancement often arise during those times. With some discipline and hard work, this house provides a great opportunity to fulfill one's ambitions using the larger global framework available to us during these periods. The tenth house symbolizes a person's connection to the world around them and how they use it to create a legacy for themselves.

House Cusps and Their Meaning

The tenth astrological house has two cusps, namely the Medium Coeli (MC) and the Imum Coeli (IC). The Medium Coeli (MC) is the point at which you reach your highest potential and signifies a person's career goals and aspirations. The Imum Coeli (IC) is the point at which you are most vulnerable and signifies the person's innermost fears and weaknesses. It is crucial to understand both cusps to gain a complete picture of the individual's career potential. The Medium Coeli encourages you to reach for the stars and strive for success, while the Imum Coeli reminds you of your limitations and helps you stay grounded in reality.

Main Keywords

The main keywords that describe the tenth house are ambition, career progression, public reputation, and social status. This house is about taking risks and achieving success through hard work and dedication. It is also about understanding how to reach one's goals by taking into consideration the larger social frameworks available to them. The tenth house is where you go to find your purpose and make your mark on the world. It is also the place where you find out how to make a name for yourself and create a lasting legacy. The keywords related to the tenth house help you to focus your energy on reaching your goals and making a difference in the world.

Description of the House's Theme

The tenth astrological house is a fascinating entity that symbolizes ambition and career progression in our lives. According to astrological beliefs, this house points to someone's social status and distinction in their chosen profession. It also reflects how individuals will find stability and satisfaction with their achievements, what goals they pursue, the focus they put into them, and the respect they receive from society. Such matters become increasingly important as someone strives to move up the ranks. You may not fully comprehend how someone's ambitions affect the cosmic plane, but the concept of the tenth house can certainly give you a better insight into the process.

Planet/Sign Analysis

Capricorn brings with it an ambition that drives you to reach the top of your chosen profession. It also teaches you how to stay focused and disciplined with your goals, as this is a necessary part of reaching success. Saturn, on the other hand, gives you a sense of responsibility and structure. It encourages you to be accountable for your actions and to understand the consequences of your decisions. Together, these two planets provide you with a sense of focus and power that you can use to reach greater heights.

In conclusion, the tenth house is a powerful and influential one. It asks you to embrace your ambitions, determine your goals and strive for them with purpose and hard work. It also teaches you the importance of discipline, structure, and responsibility in your life. Understanding these concepts can help you to achieve greater heights in your career and ambitions. With the help of the tenth house, you can create a better future for yourself and achieve your dreams. In addition, the energies of the tenth house can help you understand your position in society and how you can use that to further your ambitions. It encourages you to take risks, use the global framework available to you and make your mark on the world. You can use this astrological house to reach new heights with hard work and dedication.

The Eleventh House: Friendship

The eleventh astrological house is full of mystery, but one thing which is known about it is that it signifies friendship and social connections. This house serves as a reminder that having close friends and meaningful relationships encourages you to feel appreciated, creates enjoyable conversations, and promotes socialization. Furthermore, this astrological house emphasizes shared interests, support systems, and understanding in friendships. Whether you meet someone at college, during an outing, or even online, the eleventh house highlights the importance of building a strong connection with those around you so you can grow together in life experiences.

Ruling Zodiac Sign and Planet

Both Aquarius and Uranus rule the eleventh house. Aquarius stands for progressiveness, innovation, independence, and friendship. It encourages you to be unique, creative, and non-conforming. Furthermore, Aquarius pushes you toward thinking outside of the box and embracing your individuality. Similarly, Uranus helps you make connections and explore your environment. It is associated with technology, science, and unconventional ideas that can help you to gain a better understanding of your surroundings.

House Cusps and Their Meaning

The eleventh house cusps are between Aquarius and Pisces. The cusp of the eleventh house is associated with the theme of friendship and finding a sense of connection with those around you. As this house is associated with Aquarius, it can also be seen as the collective consciousness of the universe. It encourages you to think about your social and environmental environment and how you can work together to make a positive change in the world.

Main Keywords

The eleventh astrological house is an exciting and expansive energy that is well worth exploring. It's a unique blend of friendship, collective consciousness, socialization, technology, science, progressiveness, innovation, and independence, all merging to form a distinct identity. Filled with curious potentials and possibilities that can often go untapped, the eleventh house encourages you to explore your creativity, seek out meaningful connections with others and stay open-minded toward the new dynamics unfolding in the world around you. With the right mindset and attitude, any individual working within this house has the opportunity to experience drastic personal growth and help shape a more progressive future for everyone.

Description of the House's Theme

The eleventh astrological house is an interesting, creative, and expansive energy that symbolizes friendship and collective consciousness. This house encourages you to think outside of the box and explore your environment. You can use this house to connect with others, build meaningful relationships and open your mind to the new and innovative ideas which are constantly emerging in society. It is also a reminder that working together can make a positive change in the world and help shape a better future for all.

Planet/Sign Analysis

Aquarius, the ruling zodiac sign of the eleventh house, stands for progressiveness, non-conformity, and innovation. Aquarius encourages you to think with an open mind and explore your environment more abstractly. It also helps you gain a deeper understanding of the world around you and embrace your individuality and unique perspective.

Uranus, the ruling planet of this house, symbolizes technology, science, and unconventional ideas. This planet helps you to make connections and understand your environment more creatively. It pushes you to think outside the box and come up with innovative solutions to your challenges. By exploring your creativity, you can make a positive change in the world and create a better, brighter future for everyone.

Going beyond your comfort zone can be daunting, but the eleventh house helps you do just that. This is where you discover new ideas and build relationships with others. You can engage with people and concepts which may have been previously unknown to you and open your mind in exciting ways. It's not easy doing something different or going out of your way to befriend someone new, yet it can be incredibly rewarding in the end. Why not take a chance and see what this amazing house has to offer? You never know what you may find!

The Twelfth House: Spirituality

The twelfth astrological house is an interesting concept that often resonates with individuals looking to increase their spiritual awareness. It can serve as a map, guiding you on your journey to a greater understanding of yourself, the universe, and the divine. This house has always been associated with spirituality and offers spiritual growth through the exploration of the subconscious mind. By discovering your true intentions and goals, you strengthen your connection with the divine and are better able to recognize your true purpose in life. Through careful self-reflection, astrology offers you a gateway into deepening your spiritual practice, looking within yourself to find peace, joy, enlightenment, and, ultimately, transformation.

Ruling Zodiac Sign and Planet

The twelfth astrological house is ruled by Pisces together with its ruling planet Neptune. These two aspects are closely intertwined, as they both represent spiritual transformation, the power of dreams and creativity, and a deep connection with the divine. Pisces encourages you to look within and better understand your spiritual nature. Neptune, on the other hand, helps you find peace and fulfillment by exploring your subconscious and emotional depths.

House Cusps and Their Meaning

The twelfth house cusps are the Medium Coeli (MC), which is located at the top of the chart, and the Imum Coeli (IC) at the bottom. The MC is associated with your future goals and ambitions, helping you discover what you truly want in life and what drives you to achieve your highest potential. It also encourages you to go beyond your comfort zone and explore the unknown, opening up a world of possibilities. The IC, on the other hand, symbolizes your foundation and personal values. It encourages you to look into your past experiences to gain insight and understanding into your current reality.

Main Keywords

Everyone has fascinating dreams and thoughts that come to them from time to time. However, what is truly remarkable is the prophetic wisdom you can receive from your unconsciousness. The twelfth house of astrology teaches you how to explore your deepest subconscious levels, develop spiritual awareness, and use creativity to shape your path toward transformation. As you open up to the mystic power of this area of your life, you begin to appreciate the infinite potential of spirituality and divinity which resides within you. It's easier said than done, but there's no greater journey than taking this plunge into your inner depths and discovering a world of everlasting possibilities.

Description of the House's Theme

The twelfth house of astrology is a magical place that holds many secrets and mysteries. It speaks to the power of imagination, spirituality, and transformation. This house is deeply connected with the subconscious and offers you guidance on how to tap into the creative depths of yourself. Through careful self-reflection, spiritual practice, and exploration of your subconscious mind, you can unlock a deeper understanding of yourself and discover the true meaning of your life's journey. Ultimately, you can use this knowledge to create positive change in your life and the world around you.

Planet/Sign Analysis

The power of Pisces and Neptune in the twelfth house is profound, as they bring you to a place of deep inner understanding. Pisces reminds you to look within and take an introspective approach to gain a greater understanding of your spiritual nature. Neptune helps you to dive into your subconscious mind, accessing the powerful energy that lies within. Together, these two planets help you to unlock the deepest mysteries of your subconscious and explore realms of creativity and imagination that are often left untapped. By learning how to use the energy of Pisces and Neptune, you can open up a world of endless possibilities and find true enlightenment.

Ultimately, the twelfth house teaches you how to open up to your spiritual depths, unlock creativity and imagination, and embark on a journey of transformation and personal growth. By embracing the vast power that lies within us, we can use our insight to make positive changes in our lives and the world around us. The twelfth house is a gateway to profound spiritual wisdom and exploration, allowing you to unlock the mysteries of your subconscious and access the divine power within. You can find true enlightenment and inner peace with careful reflection and spiritual practice.

The tenth, eleventh, and twelfth houses of astrology are profoundly powerful, offering you guidance on how to access your creative potential and embark on a journey of spiritual growth. Through careful self-reflection, creative exploration, and unlocking the mysteries of your subconscious mind, you can gain a greater understanding of yourself and uncover a world of endless possibilities. With the knowledge from these houses, you can use your newfound insight to make positive changes in your life and the world around you. Uncover the power of spiritual wisdom and discover your true potential by exploring these three houses. By doing so, you can find peace, enlightenment, and a greater understanding of yourself.

Chapter 10: Putting It All Together: Your Birth Chart

Birth charts are an incredible tool to help you to better understand a person's character and life. By looking at the position of planets, luminaries, and other astrological points at the time of birth, you can get an overall sense of a person's essential nature as well as their more obvious traits and abilities. It doesn't stop there. Birth charts can be used to accurately predict events that might manifest in one's life, highlight any potential pitfalls, and suggest actions that could aid in the fulfillment of one's greatest potential. It can provide powerful advice, guidance, and words of caution for anyone who takes the time to immerse themselves in this fascinating science.

This chapter will provide a brief overview of interpreting and understanding birth charts. It will begin by defining what a birth chart is and its purpose. It will then take an example of a natal chart and discuss how to read, interpret, and draw potential conclusions from it. With the help of clear step-by-step instructions (including examples), you will better understand how to interpret the chart. The positions of planets, luminaries, and other astrological points within the chart matter greatly when interpreting birth charts. Signs, degrees, and intercepted signs on the chart can provide insight into relationships, work ethics, interests, and flaws.

What Is a Birth Chart?

A birth chart is a symbolic representation of the sky as viewed from Earth at the time of someone's birth. It is a map of the sky at the specific moment and place of your birth, offering insight into the subconscious and spiritual qualities such as personality traits, emotions, and physical looks. In addition to psychological characteristics, it can be used to better understand career paths to pursue meaningful careers which are tailored to your unique profile. Taking an in-depth look at a birth chart can be incredibly revealing simply because they provide a focal point for understanding your life, including the past, present, and future.

How to Interpret a Natal Chart

Interpreting a natal chart is a fascinating and rewarding experience since it can provide unique insights into an individual's personality. At its simplest level, a natal chart consists of various planets and points that are placed in a symbolic 360-degree wheel around the Earth. Using astrological principles, these positions can be read to reveal the potential and objectives of the individual.

First, you should look for major planetary patterns (such as trines or squares) to determine the energies which are conducive to how you interact with the world. Second, specific planet degrees will indicate particular qualities of life experience. Finally, pay attention to how the planets interact with each other - this can offer deep insight into yourself and your relationships. With practice, looking at your natal chart can unlock new layers of understanding!

A. Degrees and Intercepted Signs

A natal chart is comprised of two core components, namely degrees and intercepted signs. Degrees are measured from 0°-360° and represent the position of each planet in the sky upon your birth. Meanwhile, intercepted signs are 12-fold divisions of a sign that only appear when certain planets occupy special features or when they occupy confined constellations. However, these trapped signs don't have any essential value unless planets are present to activate them, meaning you should never rely on intercepted signs alone. With these fundamentals in mind, you can start building your very own natal chart and deciphering the pieces that make up your personality.

B. Relationship, Work Ethics, and Interests

Interpreting a natal chart can be a great way to learn more about yourself and what makes you tick. It can provide insights into your relationships with others, how you approach work, the lifestyle that suits you best, and even what interests you the most. There's no "right" or "wrong" way to interpret a natal chart. It's entirely based on subjective observations and intuitions. However, by using reliable information from an astrologer and carefully exploring all of the various aspects of your chart, such as planets and zodiac signs, an individual can begin to uncover valuable pieces of information about themselves. Whether you're just curious or in search of some serious self-reflection, learning how to interpret a natal chart is sure to bring major benefits.

C. Flaws and Qualities

Interpreting a natal chart can be intimidating because of the amount of information available and the overwhelming range of flaws and qualities to analyze. However, with a few simple guidelines, you can approach it with confidence. Start by thinking broadly. A natal chart gives you an overview of personality traits and indicators, which may lead to understanding how planetary influences affect your life. A convenient way to make sense of this is to break down a chart into pieces and gauge the effects each snapshot has on your life.

Afterward, assess which qualities are either accelerating growth and development or causing challenges and challenges that need addressing. Finally, cultivate resilience when it comes to accepting any unfavorable outcomes from a natal chart. Keep in mind that all interpretations are subjective. Qualities, regardless of how unfavorable, can provide insight into how best to use strengths by focusing on gradually building weaknesses over time.

D. Aspects and Transits

The natal chart is an essential tool used for astrological interpretation, commonly used for understanding one's personality and preferences. It utilizes the aspects and transits to tell a story about your place in the Universe. Aspects measure the angles between planets in the sky, while transits are what happens to them over time as they move through the sky from month to month and year to year. Understanding how to interpret a natal chart is the basis for gaining insight into the complex motion of planets.

Depending on which system you utilize, interpreting natal charts can encompass psychological analysis, zodiacal wisdom, or practical advice. Whatever your practice may be, studying a natal chart requires patience and dedication, as each individual's planetary movements are unique. With advanced knowledge of reading and using these tools, you can gain a holistic view of your life when you interpret your chart.

E. The Rising Sign and Its Meaning

Interpreting a natal chart can be daunting, but understanding the basics of the rising sign can make it less intimidating. A person's rising sign is calculated based on the position of the sun and other celestial bodies according to their exact birth time and place. It's important to look at all of the components together to form an interpretation. While different signs have different energies, what matters more is how they interact with each other. The rising sign helps start this process by providing insight into someone's basic personality and characteristics in addition to other deeper layers of personality. Even though it is a complex topic, learning how to interpret a natal chart doesn't need to feel overwhelming if you break it down into digestible pieces and take your time.

Tips and Tricks for Interpreting a Birth Chart

Now that you have a better understanding of how to read and interpret a natal chart, here are some tips to make the process easier.

A. Look for Patterns

Looking at your birth chart is like putting on a detective's hat. By examining all of its components, you can start to build an understanding of the energies that inform a person's life. With practice, people can develop methods for analyzing and interpreting birth charts to get information about various aspects of one's life. The more time and effort invested in this study, the deeper your appreciation and understanding of it will become. Unexpected patterns sometimes appear among these symbols, helping to provide clarity on what is going on at any given moment in a person's life. Learning to read and interpret these patterns can be incredibly rewarding.

B. Consider Sign Rulerships

Interpreting a birth chart can be a powerful practice for self-discovery. One of the most important components in birth chart interpretation is understanding sign rulerships. This means looking at which zodiac signs each planet rules and their corresponding astrological houses. For example, Mercury rules Virgo and Gemini, while Saturn rules Capricorn and Aquarius. When evaluating a birth chart, you can see how those planets impact different parts of the person's life based on the corresponding zodiac signs and houses. It's exciting to discover how the planets have influenced someone's life journey.

C. Pay Attention to Any Fixed Stars on the Chart

When interpreting a birth chart, pay special attention to any fixed stars that appear on the chart. Fixed stars are points in the night sky that exhibit an influence over world events and individual lives. Among other things, a person's birth chart is determined by the positioning of these fixed stars at the time of their birth. Knowing where a particular star resides in a person's birth chart can enrich our understanding of their life path and karma, allowing us to draw more empowering insights from the same chart.

D. Make Connections between Planets and Houses

Interpreting a birth chart can be a fun and insightful process. To start, you will need to get an overview of the key elements of a birth chart, including the planets and houses. The planets represent different energies and living areas that are believed to impact your life. These include inner planets such as the Sun, Moon, Mercury, and Venus, which symbolize our inner qualities and outward expressions, outer planets such as Jupiter, Saturn, Neptune, and Uranus, which are associated with larger patterns in your life, as well as Pluto and Chiron.

The houses represent parts of our life that are affected by these adventures. Each house has a particular focus, from relationships in the 7th house to career choices in the 10th house. Connecting these two ingredients will help you to gain insight into how planetary energies affect different aspects of life according to your birth chart.

E. Keep an Open Mind and Notice the Details

Interpreting a birth chart can be an eye-opening journey for those eager to learn more about themselves. By delving deep into the details of their astrological chart, readers can gain powerful insights into their unique lives and personalities. While it is natural to feel cautiously hesitant, keep an open mind and be willing to accept whatever discoveries come your way. With each birth chart interpreted, you can come away with precious knowledge that can help you further understand and explore different facets of their psyche. Don't be afraid to let yourself dive deep, forget preconceived notions, and find out what truly resonates with you.

F. Use Your Intuition to Develop a Symbolic Reading of the Chart

Interpreting a birth chart can provide you with deep insight into yourself and your relationships with other people. Drawing on symbols in your surrounding environment to create a meaningful interpretation of a birth chart is an incredibly valuable tool for personal growth and development. In most cases, the symbols used should have some connection with the person. That will add an extra layer of personal relevance to the task.

Harnessing the power of intuition and taking time to meditate upon the symbols chosen can be incredibly useful when interpreting a hybrid chart, allowing you to truly delve into each area of significance. Utilizing your natural senses and sensibilities will give you a renewed understanding of yourself, unlocking new realizations that could set you on an exciting path toward self-discovery.

G. Consider Aspects and Their Meaning

Instead of viewing a birth chart as a fixed and predetermined meaning, it should be seen as an opportunity to consider multiple aspects of yourself and to discover creative possibilities. When you interpret your birth chart, use the information you glean as inspiration, identify the gifts and talents which show up, learn how the stars and planets influenced them, and how your chart can guide you in living your best life. With each part of the chart having its meaning, from the planets, signs, houses, and elements, take time to research and explore what each one brings to your individual story. You can use that knowledge to understand yourself better, change patterns of behavior that no longer serve you, and discover new pathways for growth opportunities, all with a greater sense of purpose.

Reading and interpreting a birth chart is one of the oldest forms of astrological study. By delving into its symbolic meaning, you can gain a greater understanding of yourself and your unique perspective on the world. While it can be an incredibly eye-opening experience, it is essential to remain open-minded and use your intuition to develop a meaningful interpretation. By taking time to consider aspects such as planets, signs, houses, elements, and their respective meanings, you can gain a unique insight into your own life and how the stars have shaped it.

Extra: Astrological Symbols and Glyphs

A natal chart is a unique map of the sky at the exact moment you were born. It can tell you many things about yourself, and more often than not, a natal chart generated online will come with glyphs and symbols. While these images may seem daunting at first glance, have no fear. This final chapter will explain them in detail so that you can understand just what your natal chart means.

Planet Glyphs and Symbols

Have you heard of planet glyphs and symbols? These symbols are believed to be used by civilizations outside of our own, including civilizations from other galaxies. Many scientists agree that these glyphs could tell a story about the lives of forgotten people who once inhabited certain planets scattered across the cosmos. They may even provide glimpses into what the future may hold for you. Understanding planet glyphs and symbols can be difficult, but gaining insight into them can be incredibly rewarding!

Here are the most commonly used glyphs and symbols for each planet:

- Sun: A circle with a dot in the center
- Moon: A crescent moon
- Mercury: A curve above a circle with a cross at the bottom

- Venus: A circle with a cross at the bottom
- Mars: A circle with an arrow pointing up
- Jupiter: A combination of two symbols, the crescent moon and the cross
- Saturn: A cross with a curl at the bottom
- Uranus: Two half circles with a cross in the middle
- Neptune: A trident
- Pluto: A small circle with a cross underneath

Sign Glyphs and Symbols

Each sign of the zodiac has its unique glyph and symbol that can be used to represent it. These symbols have been used for thousands of years and can provide insight into a person's character, strengths, and weaknesses. From Egyptian hieroglyphs to Chinese pictograms and even modern-day road signs, these symbols have found their way into your everyday world and day-to-day life. They help you to navigate new places, and create an unambiguous understanding when using a language that isn't shared. Here are the glyphs and symbols for each sign of the zodiac:

- Aries: A ram's head
- Taurus: A bull's head
- Gemini: Two pillars
- Cancer: A crab
- Leo: A lion's head
- Virgo: A maiden
- Libra: Scales
- Scorpio: A scorpion
- Sagittarius: An archer
- Capricorn: A mountain goat
- Aquarius: Water bearer
- Pisces: Two fish

Abbreviations

When reading a natal chart, you may see some abbreviations for certain important aspects of the chart. Here is a list of some of the most common abbreviations you may come across:

- MC: Midheaven or Medium Coeli
- IC: Imum Coeli or Nadir of the chart
- ASC: Ascendant
- DSC: Descendant
- Deg: Degree
- Hs: House
- PL: Planetary Ruler
- N. Node: North Node
- S. Node: South Node
- Chiron: The Wounded Healer

Now that you understand the glyphs and symbols used in natal charts, you have all the tools to interpret your chart. With this knowledge, you will have a much better understanding of the unique story in your very own natal chart.

Conclusion

Astrology is an ancient practice that has had a resurgence of popularity in recent years! Each zodiac sign brings unique traits. The twelve signs represent the passage of the seasons and the position of planets at the time of birth. They can explain why you interact with others or yourself in certain ways. Tapping into essential energies related to each zodiac sign helps you find balance and better understand your cycles. All these aspects combine to form a detailed picture of your character.

Learning more about yourself through your zodiac sign, discovering you have a great affinity for certain traits, or uncovering a few habits that habitually cause issues in life can be a strangely gratifying experience. Everyone enjoys finding out more about themselves, and in the case of astrological signs, it can reveal dimensions to your personality that you never knew existed. With star signs divided into twelve categories based on the position of stars and planets at the time of birth, it becomes easier to understand why some things come naturally to you while others do not.

Astrology has been a part of countless cultures for centuries and remains one of the most intriguing aspects of human history. From Chinese astrology to Western zodiac signs, people have used this ancient system as a way to make important decisions and plan for the future. Technology has allowed people to access this knowledge in a matter of seconds instead of having to search through volumes of old texts or seek out an experienced astrologer.

With mobile apps and digital platforms, today's generation is privileged to have such an abundance of information at their fingertips. It's no wonder that astrology remains one of the most popular spiritual schools there. Take this informative guide, for example. It covered all the basics, including information on the planets, zodiac signs, houses, and asteroids. From the ego to home, career, and travel, every area of life is touched upon. It also provided an understanding of the symbols and glyphs used in astrology.

This book gives you a comprehensive view of the cosmic realm to help you make sense of this ancient practice and give you a chance to explore your birth chart. With the knowledge gained from this book, you can use astrology as a tool for self-growth and exploration. In doing so, you may find yourself better equipped to make important life decisions and form meaningful relationships. All in all, astrology can be a powerful guiding force in your journey toward self-discovery.

So, what are you waiting for? Start exploring your chart today and unlock the secrets to a more fulfilling life!

Here's another book by Mari Silva that you might like

Your Free Gift
(only available for a limited time)

Thanks for getting this book! If you want to learn more about various spirituality topics, then join Mari Silva's community and get a free guided meditation MP3 for awakening your third eye. This guided meditation mp3 is designed to open and strengthen ones third eye so you can experience a higher state of consciousness. Simply visit the link below the image to get started.

https://spiritualityspot.com/meditation

References

Brown, M. (2022, December 12). The 12 houses of astrology, explained. InStyle. https://www.instyle.com/12-houses-of-astrology-6890300

Kelly, A. (2018, October 6). What Houses in your birth chart mean, and how to find them. Allure. https://www.allure.com/story/12-astrology-houses-meaning

Lanyadoo, J. (2019, August 19). Here's everything you need to know about astrology houses. Cosmopolitan. https://www.cosmopolitan.com/lifestyle/a28700440/astrology-houses/

Mazurek, D. (2022, November 16). What do the 12 houses mean in astrology? Dictionary.com. https://www.dictionary.com/e/what-do-the-houses-mean-in-astrology/

The Editors of Encyclopedia Britannica. (2022). zodiac. In Encyclopedia Britannica.

Tomar, D. (2019, May 30). Learn about the 12 houses in Vedic astrology. AstroTalk Blog - Online Astrology Consultation with Astrologer; AstroTalk. https://astrotalk.com/astrology-blog/houses-in-vedic-astrology/

Wright, J. (2022, January 2). What are the 12 houses of astrology? PureWow. https://www.purewow.com/wellness/12-houses-of-astrology

Printed in Great Britain
by Amazon